Senior Women: How to Make The Extra Money You Need

Helen Hunt and Paula Sanderson

Parker Publishing Company, Inc.

West Nyack, New York

© 1984, *by*

PARKER PUBLISHING COMPANY, INC.

West Nyack, N. Y.

Library of Congress Cataloging in Publication Data

Hunt, Helen.
  Senior women.

  Includes bibliographies and index.
    1. Aged women--Employment--United States.
  2. Part-time employment--United States. I. Sanderson,
  Paula. II. Title.
  HD6056.2.U6H86   1984   650.1'4'0240565   84-1130

ISBN 0-13-806570-5
ISBN 0-13-806562-4 {PBK}

Printed in the United States of America

PREFACE

This book was written to help senior women find ways to supplement their social security checks or other pension income and lift their lives from an impoverished level to the more secure level of having spending money once again in their pockets.

In 1984, the amount allowed by the Social Security Administration for earned income was $6,960 for those 65 years of age or older without loss of any benefits. Because there are so many different ways to make this amount, this book explains in great detail how to make this extra money to supplement your social security benefits.

A step-by-step procedure of each project outlines what to do, how to do it, and most important of all—how to sell your projects once they are done and ready for marketing. Most of these small business ideas are home-based careers that can be undertaken by both experienced and inexperienced women. Some apply to shut-ins and handicapped women.

At the end of the book are sections on finding financial help in starting a new business. General information that answers the questions most asked at the Social Security offices is supplied here, as well as information on how the new tax laws affect the earnings on the interest and dividends you might be receiving; names and addresses to write to if you need help from the government; information about senior citizens' associations, banking hints, home repairs made easy, common investment and financial problems, and much more.

This information is given with many words of encouragement. There are examples of successes by women who have started a small, home-based business with no previous experience, only with a strong need for extra money.

FACTS

According to the Women's Bureau of the U.S. Department of Labor, the average woman worker earns only about three-fifths of what the average man does. Full-time working minority women fared even worse. Older single women fared the worst of all, and they are among the poorest people in our nation today. Most women over the age of 65 depend solely on their social security benefits for survival.

The economic security a woman 65 or older has comes from earned income over a selected period of time, whether she is now widowed, or divorced, or has never married.

The average woman worker is as well educated as the average man. The more education a woman has, the more likely she is to work. Among women with four years of college, three out of five are in the labor force.

Statistics also tell us that 90 out of 100 women who reach the age of 65 are flat broke!

TABLE OF CONTENTS

Preface 5

PART I   QUICK AND EASY MONEY-MAKING PROJECTS

Chapter 1   NEEDLEWORK. 15
Knitted Mitten Duster · Eyeglass
Case · Windsocks · Pretty Place Mats with
Matching Napkin Holders · Coupon
Wallets · Place Mat Purses · Book Carrier and
Cover

Chapter 2   CRAFTS FOR THE HANDICAPPED. 26
Shell Craft · Canvas Embroidery · Rosette
Craft · Square Needlework

Chapter 3   CLEVER HANDCRAFTS. 34
Flower Garden Sachets · Pomander
Balls · Glass Painting · Decoupage and
Collage · Seashell Crafts · Shell-Decorated
Mirrors · Sandcasting · Hand-Shaped
Candles · Bayberry Candles · Hand Printing on
Fabric · Weaving · Leatherwork ·
Papermaking Using Junk Mail · Custom Party
Favors for Children

Chapter 4   WALLPAPERING—WHO, ME?. 67
Types of Wall Coverings · Prepasted Wallpaper:
The Number One Choice for

Beginners · Removing Old Paper · General
Preparation

Chapter 5   TYPING RÉSUMÉS FOR A STEADY INCOME . . . 74

Chapter 6   IF I CAN GET 30 CENTS FOR EMPTY CANS
             HOW COME I'M WATCHING THE SOAPS? 78

Chapter 7   GROWING CACTUS—EASY TO GROW, EASY
             TO SELL 80

PART II   LOOKING AHEAD: WHAT TO DO—AND HOW TO
             DO IT!

Chapter 8   HOW TO SELL FOR PROFIT 85
             Deciding on the Selling
             Price · Self-Promotion · How to Get an Order

Chapter 9   CONSIDERING A DIRECT-SALES JOB 88
             Direct Sales · Direct Sales Firms

Chapter 10   STARTING YOUR OWN MAIL ORDER
             BUSINESS! 93
             Starting Out · Choosing Your Product · Buying
             a Product for Resale · Advertising Your
             Product · Keeping Business Records

Chapter 11   DECORATING FOR DOLLARS 99
             Simplified Use of Color

Chapter 12   IF YOU CAN PAINT, EXTRA DOLLARS ARE
             YOURS! 103
             How to Show Your Paintings · How to Price
             Your Paintings · Should You Mat or
             Frame? · Commissioned Paintings

Chapter 13   CUSTOMIZED POSTAL SERVICE 106

Chapter 14   COSMETOLOGY FOR DOLLARS IN YOUR OWN
             HOME 109
             Checking Your Home · Building Up a

Clientele · Equipment · Financing · Satisfied
Customers · Retailing Beauty Aids · New
Developments · Pampering Your
Client · Trends

Chapter 15   MODERNIZING THE FLOWER BUSINESS...... 114
Interior Plantscaping

Chapter 16   PLANTS FOR RENT........................ 116
A Beginner's Basic Inventory

Chapter 17   SMALL FAMILY DAY CARE CENTER IN YOUR
HOME 120
Licensing

Chapter 18   YOUR HOUSE OR APARTMENT—HOW EXTRA
SPACE MEANS EXTRA MONEY.............. 123
How to Determine the Weekly Rate · Some
Pitfalls · Your House Is Your Castle!

Chapter 19   PROPERTY MANAGEMENT—FREE TIME IS
PROFIT!................................... 128
How Much Is the Rent? · Showing the
Apartment · Leases · Late-Paying
Tenant · Deposits · Standard Management
Fees

Chapter 20   THE HANDCRAFTS BUSINESS: TURN A PART-
TIME PLEASURE INTO A FULL-TIME PROFIT . 135
Production in Your Home · Equipment and
Materials · Financing · Government
Assistance · Looking Ahead · How Will You
Price Your Craft? · Ready to Sell? · Craft Fairs
and Art Shows · Street Exhibits

Chapter 21   HOW YOU CAN TEACH SEWING 142
How to Find Your Students · How Much to
Charge · Trends · Hints on Pampering Your
Students

Chapter 22   HOW TO TEACH NEEDLECRAFT. 146
              How to Pamper Your Needlecrafters

Chapter 23   DISCOUNT CLOTHES FOR CHILDREN. 148

PART III   BEFORE YOU SEND FOR THE REPAIRMAN . . .

              Television · Refrigerator · Gas Stove · Electric
              Range · Tender Loving Care for Your Car

PART IV   THE GOVERNMENT: HOW IT CAN SAVE YOU
              MONEY, HOW IT CAN MAKE YOU MONEY

Chapter 24   TELESERVICE. 161

Chapter 25   SOCIAL SECURITY. 163
              Questions and Answers · Your Right to Appeal
              Under Social Security or Medicare ·
              Supplemental Security Income (SSI) What You
              Should Know About It and How to Obtain
              It · Hospital and Medicare Made New Changes
              in Medicare · How Farm Income Affects Your
              Social Security Benefits

Chapter 26   TAXES 181
              Property Tax Assistance for Senior Citizens and
              Blind/Disabled Persons · Tax Advantages for
              Seniors

Chapter 27   TAKING CARE OF YOUR MONEY. 185
              Checking Account Tips · Using Direct Deposit

Chapter 28   STARTING YOUR OWN BUSINESS WITH HELP
              FROM THE SMALL BUSINESS
              ADMINISTRATION 188

Chapter 29   A PART-TIME JOB FROM THE JOBS TRAINING
              PARTNERSHIP ACT (JTPA). 192

Appendix A HELPFUL HINTS FROM YOUR SENIOR
CITIZENS ASSOCIATION 193

Appendix B SUCCESS STORIES 196

Index 201

1

Quick and Easy
Money-Making Projects

1

NEEDLEWORK

KNITTED MITTEN DUSTER

Knit your way to extra money while watching the soap operas and using up all your odds and ends of yarn!

What is it? It is a mitten? No—it's a duster! Slip the duster over your hand and whisk it over tables, chairs, and delicate bric-a-brac.

The dust clings to the many strands until you are finished dusting. Then just shake it out and, once in a while, toss it into the washing machine. Anyone who can knit and purl simple items can knit the duster. Use thick nylon yarn and large needles to do the job fast. You can really go mad with gorgeous colors!

Materials

2 oz. Quik-knit bulky nylon yarn (supermarkets, knitting shops, and five-and-dime stores carry it for about $1.10), a pair of #10 knitting needles (about $1), a #10 crochet hook (about 85¢).

Directions

1. Cuff: Cast on 30 stitches, knit 2, purl 2 for the ribbing (3").
2. Body: First row, knit; second row, purl; continue for 6 inches. Continue plain knitting each row for 2 inches.
3. Shaping off: Remove 15 stitches on stitch holder (a large safety pin will do). Continue knitting each row, casting off 1 stitch at the beginning of each row 3 times. Cast off remaining 9 stitches. Pick up stitches on holder and repeat as above. With matching yarn, sew seams together in mitten shape.
4. Making strands: Cut a pice of cardboard 2½" wide and wind yarn lightly around it. Wind about 20 times, then cut one side of yarn, making 5" strands.
5. Knotting strands: Fold strand in half. With crochet hook, pull folded end through the body stitch and hook loose ends through the loop to knot. Starting at the seam, knot a strand into every other stitch, forming the dusting palm. Continue every other row to top.

Note: If you are an expert mitten knitter and comfortable with four needles, you might prefer knitting the duster your own way. Just follow the stitch and size directions.

How to Sell

Make up a few dusters in ravishing colors and see your local boutique, gift shop, or hardware store owner. With Quik-knit yarn and large needles you can easily make five dusters a week, even while watching TV.

Sell them for at least $4 each—an extra thousand dollars a year for you!

You may want to look into selling your projects on *consignment*, which means that the store may keep one-third of the selling price and give you the other two-thirds when the item is sold. Agreement on the selling price and percentage can be flexible between you and the store owner, but keep a record of the number, color, and other pertinent information about your projects.

EYEGLASS CASE

Sit in an armchair and handsew your way to extra dollars!

If you are handicapped, if you cannot buzz away on a sewing machine, or if you just like to sew by hand while chatting with a friend, making these eyeglass cases is for you!

Materials

Two 8" sqares of material. For the case: Satin, brocade, velvet, anything flowered or pretty. For the lining: felt or heavy flannel.

Note: Friends and thrift shops can be the sources of discarded evening and drapery material. Fabric shops usually have little squares of felt for sale in many colors. Have fun with touches of lace, beads, and appliqués.

Directions

1. Place an 8" square of satin and an 8" square of felt together, wrong sides out. Fold in half. Round off the top as illustrated.

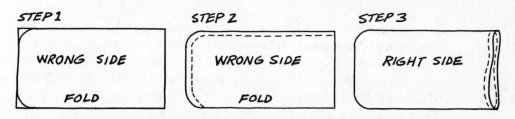

2. Separate the pieces and again fold each piece in half, wrong side out. Sew up the curved and the long, open side of both pieces. Sew the seams so the case is 3½" wide for large glasses. You can measure average and smaller glasses for size and stitch some of each.

3. Turn the satin case right side out. Cut ¼" off the open end of the lining. Still wrong side out, fit it inside the satin case. Fold the edge of the satin case to fit over the lining and hem the two edges together.

How to Sell

A basket of glorious eyeglass cases in your local boutique, drug store, or gift shop will send the dollars in your direction! The shop can take them to sell on consignment.

WINDSOCKS

Guaranteed to brighten up any dull corner of a home or apartment, windsocks also accent a patio, garden, or party area. Hang from the ceiling inside or from a tree branch outside.

A windsock is a long, cylindrical, colorful tube, made by sewing (or glueing if you can't sew) two to three bright panels of material together. The finished length is approximately two feet (different lengths hung together are interesting), and eight inches in diameter. Florist wire is inserted in the top casing to keep it from flattening. Like a wind tunnel that air blows through, a windsock has cloth openings at both ends to catch any breeze.

Vary the sizes of the color panels used in the body of the windsock. Never think in terms of two halves. If you use only two panels to make the total length, make one panel one-third the length and the other panel two-thirds (see directions that follow).

Windsock materials need body to hang properly. Select materials from remnants of drapery fabric, felt, all upholstery fabric, bed sheets (if they are unused and still have the sizing), and Indian design materials. Check at local fabric shops for odds and ends in bold colors. If you decorate your windsock with appliqués (a wonderful idea), do it before you sew up the windsock. When it is finished, you might want to trim it further with bells, beads, or shiny polyester ribbons.

Materials and Cost

One ball of variegated yarn (for two fat tassels) ($1.80); two or three panels of fabric for a total measurement of 14″ wide by 24″ long ($2); fabric glue (if you don't sew) ($2); two yards of polyester ribbon (optional) ($1); florist wire (five yards for $1).

Directions

1. Sew or glue all of the horizontal seams.
2. Form the cylinder by stitching or glueing the center seam.
3. Fold the bottom edge under ½″. Cut a ribbon streamer 1′ long. Fold the ribbon over one-fourth and sew on the inside of the cylinder every 2 or 3 inches as you stitch the hem.
4. Fold the top under ¼″, and again ½″. Stitch, but leave 1½″ to form the wire casing. Insert the wire through the casing. Trim wire and tuck inside casing.
5. Wrap all colors at once 30 times around a checkbook. Insert a 10″ double strand of yarn under the wrapped yarn. Tie tightly at the top end. Clip open the other end. Trim off all of the uneven ends.
6. Take off the checkbook, squeezing the yarn tightly around the tied end; wrap it securely with a different color yarn. Thread the end of a needle and pull it through tassel. Trim uneven ends.
7. For the handle, cut two 1″ strands over the double length desired. Twist lightly and fold in half.
8. Tie the tassels to each end of the twisted yarn. Attach to the windsock as shown on page 20.

How to Sell

A windsock, decorated gaily, made inexpensively, and priced at about $15, will sell at art shows, craft shows, boutiques, and gift shops.

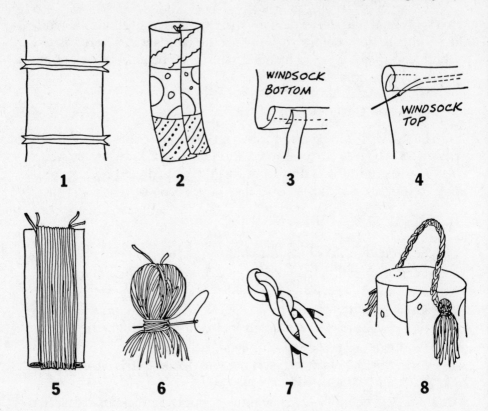

1   **2**   **3**   **4**

5   **6**   **7**   **8**

PRETTY PLACE MATS
WITH MATCHING NAPKIN HOLDERS

Here is a wonderfully successful item that you can make at home with or without a sewing machine.

If you can use your hands and need something to do with your time, making place mats is for you. It's fun and can be profitable if you carefully select the patterns that you buy, and make neat, orderly, small stitches by hand.

Materials and Cost

Quilted Material: One yard (36 × 45) will make four place mats plus four matching napkins. Cost: $5 per yard.

Unquilted Material:	One yard (36 × 54) will make four place mats plus four matching napkins plus four napkin holders. Cost: $3 per yard.
Batting:	Cost: $3 per yard.
Reversible Quilted Material:	Cost: $9 per yard.
Assorted Trims:	White or ecru lace; contrasting ribbons; ruffles made from the same or a contrasting colored fabric; bias tapes (be careful that you don't stretch the fabric as you go around the corners).

Be original and shop around for ideas of what you want to do. You might think about all of the wonderful holiday patterns that can be worked up into seasonal motifs—patterns for Thanksgiving with turkeys or pumpkins; holly berries or Santas on plain place mats in red or green colors for Christmas; Valentine's Day could be an all red fabric with a large lace heart sewn in the middle. Also consider wedding motifs, children's patterns, or sophisticated and modern colors and prints. Be creative when you use patterns and material. Take your striking saleable product into any boutique or gift shop, which will be delighted to handle it for you, and reap three to four times your cost!

COUPON WALLETS

The newest item in gift stores—here's how to make this much-in-demand coupon wallet, which is guaranteed to make grocery shopping more efficient.

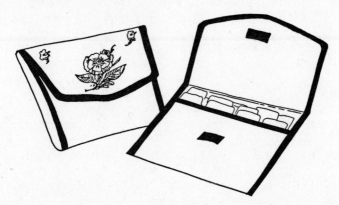

Materials and Cost

One piece of 8″ × 16″ quilted fabric ($5 per yard); two 1″ pieces of Velcro ($2 per yard); one package of wide bias tape ($2 for 2 yards); one package of standard 4″ × 6″ index cards with tabs (which can be cut down to fit) (79¢); appliqués of roses, daisies, or other objects.

Directions

Back the white side of the quilted fabric with a contrasting print, nonquilted fabric. Round off the top edges of the quilted and nonquilted fabrics. Stitch them together. Bind the sides with bias tape. Put the Velcro on the outside for the bottom piece, and on the inside for the top flap. Sew the bottom third to the middle section, leaving one-third of the finished fabric to fold down.

Quilted fabrics come in a variety of colors. Many are already backed with a complementary color or print. If the batting is too thick, remove some of it from the middle panel. Binding the curving corners is a common problem, as some of the corners will just not lie flat. If you take care not to stretch the tape and ease the tape as it is being pinned around the corners, this problem will be solved. Place the pins close together, and slightly ease the tape as you go around the corners; however, your tape should be stretched slightly on the inner curve, or it might start puckering.

Type or hand print the tabs on the index cards with the most popular items: dairy products, meats, vegetables, canned goods, pet foods, beverages, cereals, cake mixes, cleaning materials, frozen foods, and so on. Different colored index cards can be purchased at stationery and dime stores. You won't need a sewing machine to make this great little item, as it can be made just as easily by hand!

How to Sell

Fabric shops, boutiques, and gift shops should pay you $4 for each and sell them for $8 and up. Be your own business tycoon and advertise them yourself!

PLACE MAT PURSES

Place mat purses are wonderful for the summer, oh-so-easy to make, washable, sturdy, and colorful!

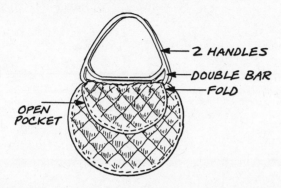

Carry this clever purse everywhere you go. The extra pockets on each side are just the thing for glasses (since it's padded), keys, and anything else you want to save time looking for. Since this purse is fully washable, and can be made in a variety of colors, it will complement all your summer clothes and even go to the seashore with you.

Materials

Two reversible 13″ × 18″ place mats ($2.50 each—or make your own); two plastic handles ($1.25 each—or substitute a shoulder strap that you can make out of material that matches the placemat). The handles are available in fabric and yarn shops.

Place mats come in a wide range of colors, so you can buy them in checks, plaids, and complementary solids and prints.

Directions

Fold down one place mat 6″ from the top. This will make a 12″ purse. Stitch the two place mats together. Slip the folded top through the double bar of the handle and stitch around the edges, leaving a 4″ opening on one side. This opening becomes the pocket and is deep enough to carry glasses safely.

How to Price:

These place mat purses are currently selling in shops for about $25.

BOOK CARRIER AND COVER

Stitch up dollars on your sewing machine!

Book lovers will want your handy book carrier, made of denim or quilted fabric. Monogram plain denim with press-on initials, or accent floral or plaid fabric with bright binding. Obtain everything at your fabric store—and start fast and easy stitching!

Materials and Cost

Heavy denim (about $2.50 per yard) or quilting (about $2.70 per yard) fabric; 1″ wide tape; ½″ wide tape.

Directions for Paperback Book Carrier

1. Cut material 17″ × 9″.
2. Roll ¼″ hem all around and stitch.
3. Fold ends in 3″ and pin or baste 3 outer sides.
4. Handles: Cut 1″ tape into two 12″ lengths. Fold ends in ½″ and pin each end 2″ from each side of cover (see illustrations). Stitch the 3 pinned sides, including the tape. You now have an open pocket to slip the paperback cover in.

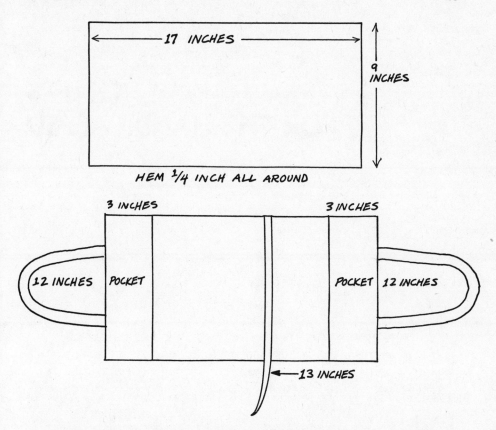

Bookmark: Cut a 13″ length of the ½″ tape and 1″ from the center.

Note: For small hardcover books, cut fabric 15″ × 10½″. For large hardcover books, cut fabric 17″ × 11½″.

How to Sell

See your local bookstores, gift shops, and card shops. Show them your samples. Estimated costs are heavy denim: $2.49 per yard; quilting: $5.50 per yard. One yard of 45″ material makes ten carriers. Thus, one carrier costs 25¢ in denim or 60¢ in quilting, plus a few cents for handles and marker. You have a nice profit per carrier if your approximate selling price is $4.50. And remember—remnant counters are for you—haunt them! These carriers are fast to make and fast to sell—you should easily make an extra $100 a month!

2

CRAFTS
FOR THE HANDICAPPED

If you are disabled, you may need to adapt your handiwork to your specific handicap. Eyes that cannot see fine stitches, hands that cannot hold work, a loss of mobility—these are specific reasons for adaption.

The crafts in this chapter are for saleable items that can make you money, and they are designed with the limitations of handicaps in mind. For instance, if you have always enjoyed needlepoint, but now have an eye problem, shell craft could be for you.

SHELL CRAFT

Shell Craft Boxes

Materials

Nests of small boxes (from a craft shop—usually six to a set); small bags of white sand; bags of assorted shells; white glue and brush; lacquer (optional).

Directions

1. Using newspaper to protect your work table, paint one surface of your box with white glue. Immediately sprinkle the wet surface with sand.

2. When the glue is dry, shake off the excess loose sand. By working on a newspaper (or tray), you can recover the excess sand. Continue sprinkling sand on the other surfaces of the box, until all sides are covered.

3. While the sanded boxes are drying, work on your sea shell designs. If you can draw the dimensions of your box on a piece of paper, you can move your shells around within it and try different designs in border and flower patterns.

4. When the sand is dry, glue the shells onto the boxes according to your designs.

5. When the decorated box is dry, it is best to spray it with clear lacquer. The lacquer will fix the sand and shells permanently in place.

Warning: To avoid inhaling dangerous fumes, lacquer spraying should be done outdoors on a protective newspaper.

How to Sell

This lovely shell craft can be sold in a boutique for a dressing table, desk top, or coffee table.

CANVAS EMBROIDERY

If your eyes are now comfortable only with large stitches, you will enjoy canvas embroidery!

According to the degree of sight loss, canvas can be used in the 3-to-5-hole-per-square-inch size. You are now into rugs or wall hangings with 6-ply yarn. If you lack feeling in the fingers, there is a plastic canvas that can be cut to size, so rigid that it will not pull out of shape.

Materials

1. Needles: For hanging or rug making, needles should have rounded points and an eye large enough for the yarn. These are usually called *tapestry needles*.
2. Frame: If you have difficulty holding your work, a frame can be made by simply nailing together four pieces of wood into a rectangle. Many types of frames can be bought, some with stands. For someone with limited mobility in the hands, one type is useful—a form that rotates on a central stand and locks into position. A wooden picture frame can be used and the canvas stretched on with drawing pins. If it is easier to work with no frame at all, the work can later be stretched and dampened. (See directions for blocking in the following pages.)
3. Yarns: Almost any yarn can be used for rugs and hangings as long as the 1-, 2- or more ply strands are thick enough to cover the canvas threads. Tapestry yarn is expensive, but it can be found in a wide range of artistic colors. Six-ply rug yarn, plastic raffia, and a nylon product (consult your supplier) can be used for rug canvas. Any needlepoint book will give you directions for many different stitches, but the easiest stitch—straight up and down from hole to adjoining hole—is the Gobelin stitch.

Design

Because of the large-holed canvas, geometric designs or stripes in canvas needlework are best. You can use graph paper, one square equaling one stitch. Fill in the design with a felt pen, and then count only the holes for the stitches. For a simple design, you can work directly on the canvas without a pattern. If you are unsure of your ability to design, simply find an artistic design and copy it.

Color

Skill in canvas embroidery is just a matter of simple stitches, so the most important factor in creating a beautiful piece is color. If you are not sure of your ability to blend colors, look at a piece of flowered fabric or a piece of wallpaper that appeals to you. Note the important color, the proportion of the colors in the flowers and leaves, the juxtaposition of shades, then your blending of color will be professional. If your eyesight is your weakness, avoid zigzags and stripes in vivid colors. Remember that the larger the scale of the design, the easier the pattern will be to work out.

Hints for Disability

1. Attach the canvas to the wooden frame with drawing pins (thumbtacks will pop out).
2. Work in two movements—bringing the needle up once through the canvas, once down.
3. To avoid dropping the needle, use double yarn, double after threading, and knot the ends. Just calculate the ply—for instance, 2-ply yarn doubled and knotted gives you 4-ply yarn for working. You can also use the yarn single, but knotted at the needle eye.

Blocking

If you find your finished work is somewhat out of shape, you can block (damp stretch) it. Take a large board, bigger than your embroidery. Place the top end of the stitching in a straight line on the board. Now tack it to the board through the stitches with drawing pins.

Pin the opposite end through the last row of stitches, stretching it so that it is parallel to the top end. Pin the sides to the board, again stretching to shape. Sprinkle water over the stretched area, so it is damp but not soaked, and *let it dry for a few days*. Your work will then be in shape, and all the edges will be even.

Rugs and wall hangings are the most appealing items in canvas needlepoint. Rugs can be made scatter size—36″ × 53″. The canvas is bought to size. Stripes and squares can be sewn together for larger sizes. You can also make cushions, jacket pockets, collars, arm patches, belts, pin cushions, spectacle cases, book covers, needle cases, and bookmarks.

Preparing Your Needlecraft for Use

Your canvas rug or hanging should have a backing. Hessian cloth (consult your fabric store—or use any heavy material), cut an inch larger than your embroidery, should be tucked in at the edges and hemmed neatly to the canvas back with matching thread. Felt makes an excellent heat-protective backing for table mats. You can cut the felt slightly smaller and glue it to the back of the embroidery (craft shops carry the proper glue).

ROSETTE CRAFT

With Rosettes, you can make balls, animals, or dolls out of scraps of material that you already have or can beg from friends. If you can sew with a needle and a thread, this is the craft for you.

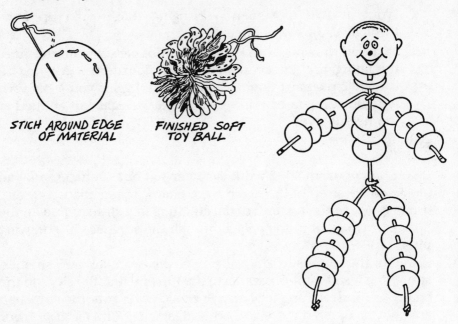

STICH AROUND EDGE
OF MATERIAL

FINISHED SOFT
TOY BALL

Materials

1. a 5½" circle to trace. Use cardboard, a dish, a jar, or anything you can use as a pattern;
2. a felt-tipped pen and scissors;
3. a needle and regular thread;
4. fine round elastic;
5. a needle with a sharp point and large eye for the elastic.

Directions for Making a Ball

1. Place your circle pattern on your material and outline with the felt-tipped pen. You will need about 40 circles. You can alternate cutting and sewing as you plan your colors.
2. Using a double sewing cotton, strongly knotted at the end, stitch around the circle with medium stitches about one

quarter inch from the edge. Then pull the thread tightly and fasten the gathering well. This forms your rosette.

3. With the large-eye needle, thread the rosettes on to the elastic. Tie the elastic tightly to form the ball, leaving the ends as a hanger.

How to Make a Rosette Doll

This is the elastic pattern for stringing the rosettes in the doll. To make the dolls's head, cut a circle of pink or white material 7" in diameter. Stitch and gather as for a rosette, but before closing, stuff it with toy filling (kapok, foam chips, or old washed nylon hosiery). For an older child, paste on eyes, nose, and mouth cut out from felt. For a younger child, draw the features with a marking pen (no loose ends for babies). For an older child, bells can be sewn at the ends of arms and legs (no bells for a baby). This will look like a boy doll, so for an older child, paste on felt ears. Again, for a baby, draw the ears with a marking pen. Attach the happy face firmly to the body.

Assembling the Rosettes on the Elastic:

1. Legs—9½" long (first elastic).
2. Body—14" long (second elastic). Knot midway at the legs. Thread double through the rosettes to 3½". Separate elastic for the arms.
3. Tie (third elastic) another piece of elastic at the arm separation, and thread double through the rosettes for the neck.

SQUARE NEEDLEWORK

If you have always knitted or crocheted, there are items to be made, even with failing eyes or shaky hands. The easiest work for these disabilities is making items with squares. Many items can be made—afghans, cushions, sweaters, purses—but start with a soft play ball!

Soft Play Ball

Do you have a bag of leftover yarns? Select six pretty colors and arrange to use the same ply for each color. If you need to use up fine yarn and thick yarn, double or triple the thin yarn to match the thick yarn. If you must get new yarn, supermarkets have sales in nylon in bright colors (.89 to 1.09). Use knitting needles with stitches large enough for your eyes (.69 to .89).

You will knit 6 squares, each of a different color. Stitch 4 squares together, lengthwise. Stitch 1 square on each side of the second square. Before you stitch the last seam, turn right side out and stuff the ball with toy filling. When firmly full, stitch the opening together.

Clutch Purse

If you can both knit and crochet, knit a square 6″ × 6″. Fold up one side of the square 3″. With a pretty contrasting color, crochet the sides together, double crocheting up along the flap and down the other side. You can crochet two loops on the flap for the two pretty buttons you will sew on.

Knitting your squares 6½″ × 6½″ and folding up 3″ is a perfect size for a checkbook and coupons en route to the supermarket.

Knitted or Crocheted Bag

Just as you used to make afghans, knit or crochet 32 squares about 5½″ × 5½″. Sew 16 of the squares together into 1 square, and 16 into another square. On the wrong side, sew together the bottoms of the two squares, then sew up the sides, leaving an opening of 1½ squares for the gusset. Turn the bag to the right side and slide one side of the bag through the opening of a wooden handle (craft or knitting shop $2–3), and hem stitch it to the inside of the bag. The size of the handle will determine the soft shirring. Repeat on the other side.

A knitted or crocheted bag should be lined. Cut the lining a little larger than the bag. Stitch the sides to match the opening gusset of the bag. With the raw edges of the lining turned into the bag, stitch the lining to the tip of the bag and along the sides. Try to use lining and thread that closely matches the color of the bag.

Tips for the Handicapped Craftsperson

Disability does not mean the end of creative potential. Many handicapped persons are able to produce craftwork of high quality and design.

Often when a person is too handicapped to continue a skilled craft, another craft can be learned and substituted. Older people with minor disabilities, such as failing eyesight or arthritic hands, usually need only adjust their expertise to their handicap.

Keep in mind the following suggestions:

1. A comfortable chair by a window with good natural light is essential. The eyes can then be rested occasionally by looking out of the window.

2. If natural light is not available, use an angle-poise lamp directed toward the craft.

3. If a table is necessary, there are cantilevered tables adjustable for height and portable.

4. The undertaking should not be too demanding. Energy must be gauged so that the craft will display good workmanship and design.

5. Avoid working too long—tiredness leads to mistakes. A mistake should always be corrected for true satisfaction, but it should be undertaken when energy is at a high.

6. An expert in any craft, such as an expert knitter, should not compromise by producing inferior work. It is better to learn another craft suited for that particular handicap.

3

CLEVER HANDCRAFTS

FLOWER GARDEN SACHETS

If you have a garden, you can make little bags of fragrance from antique recipes!

Yes, little muslin bags, tied with a velvet bow—and holding fragrant mixtures that women in Elizabethan days made to perfume their linens or to keep away moths. Every gift shop and every antique shop will want to keep a basket of these delights to sell for you. Friends and neighbors will want them, especially if you attach a little card telling of the origin of the fragrance.

For Linens

Start by collecting petals of roses or other flowers. Because many roses today have no fragrance, you will later add some oil of roses to the mixture.

Materials

You will need about 18 cups of dried flower petals, 2 cups of orris root powder, ⅓ cup cinnamon, ⅓ cup caraway, ⅓ cup mace, ⅓ cup cloves, 6 tonka beans (chopped), and 8 drops of oil of roses.

Directions

Pick fresh blossoms in midmorning on a sunny day when the dew has evaporated or in the late afternoon before the dew falls. A drying rack can consist of an old window screen laid across chair backs, or an old sheet stretched taut between two chairs. Pull off the petals and spread them one row deep across the rack. A dark, dry attic is perfect; otherwise, put them in any room where they will not blow in a draft. Let the petals dry about ten days, until they are crunchy. Store them in a bone-dry container with a tight lid. Add petals as you dry them and, if the container is glass, store in the dark.

Meanwhile, make up little 2″ × 2″ muslin bags. Buy a yard of muslin, cut pieces 2½″ by 5½″. Fold in half and stitch the two sides together. Stitch a hem in the top and run a pretty ribbon through for a drawstring. This recipe will fill about twenty-four bags.

When the ingredients are ready, chop them together into a coarse powder. Add 8 drops of oil of roses. Mix thoroughly and store in an airtight plastic bag. Let the mixture ripen a few days, shaking daily. Fill the bags and tie tightly with the ribbon. This recipe will fill about 24 bags. If you wish, tie on a little card stating that this is an antique recipe from Yorkshire, England, for perfuming linens.

To Protect Against Moths

This old European recipe has an exquisite fragrance—and also keeps away moths!

Materials

Four cups of dried rose or flower petals, ⅔ cup orrisroot powder, 2 cups vetiver, ⅔ cup ground cloves, 1 cup cedar powder, 4 drops oil of roses.

Directions

Mix all ingredients well and cure for two weeks in a sealed plastic bag, shaking daily, and then fill the little muslin bags.

Always seal each sachet in an airtight plastic bag to keep the scent strong and fresh while you are selling them.

Note: Add up the cost of the spices and rose oil. Divide the cost by the amount used per recipe to arrive at the selling price, which should be at least twice the cost of the materials.

Where to Obtain Your Ingredients

First use your supermarket spice shelf. A drug store should have
the orrisroot powder. A health food store should carry all the herb
powders. If you are still missing some ingredients and cannot find
them anywhere else, you can buy them by writing for catalogues
from the following:

> Aphrodesia Products
> 28 Carmine Street
> New York, New York 10014
>
> Capriland's Herb Farm
> Silver Street
> Coventy, Connecticut 06238
>
> Hove Parfumeur
> 723 Toulouse Street
> New Orleans, Louisiana 70130

POMANDER BALLS

*Anyone who can buy an orange can make a pomander ball—an
old-fashioned scented ball to hang in closets for fragrance.
Your gift shop will sell them fast!*

Materials

A firm, ripe orange; orrisroot powder (drug store); pumpkin pie
spice (supermarket); hairpins; gold or silver cord for hanging; rib-

bon, narrow velvet or satin for bows; decorations of choice; whole cloves (supermarket).

Directions

1. With a fork, pierce the orange skin in rows about ¼" apart.
2. In a bowl: place 3 tablespoons of pumpkin pie spice mix and 1 tablespoon of orrisroot powder. Mix thoroughly.
3. Roll the pierced fruit in the spices and lay on a dish. Into each pierced hole push a whole clove (using a thimble makes it easy to push) until the orange is closely covered with cloves.
4. For the hanger, insert a hairpin into the orange over a length of gold cord or velvet ribbon. As the fruit dries, the hairpin will hold the hanger firmly.
5. To dry: The pomander balls should now be placed on a cake rack or screen for free circulation of air, top and bottom. Leave in a cool room for two or three weeks.
6. When the ball feels hard as a stone, you can decorate—letting your imagination go wild with pretty velvet, gold or silver cord, artificial holly, pearls, sequins.
7. When finished, wrap each pomander ball in a plastic sandwich bag or plastic wrap tied firmly with a ribbon.

How to Sell

Take a number of pomander balls wrapped in plastic and placed in a tight covered box to your gift shop. Keep out one or two pomander balls for display in the shop. The display balls can be renewed from time to time. The orrisroot powder is made from Florentine iris and the combination with spices is longlasting, but the pomander ball should be kept in plastic until ready to hang.

Pomander balls—as sweet as the extra dollars coming your way!

GLASS PAINTING

Take any glass object—a tumbler, a vase, a storage jar—and transform it into a thing of beauty in a few easy steps.

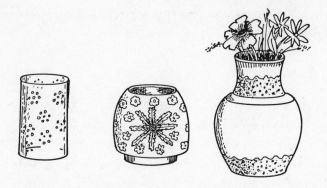

You don't have to be a trained artist to paint simple designs, and you need only a few inexpensive materials. If you start with a simple design (see illustration), you will soon move on to painted bathroom sets, kitchen sets, bar glasses, and desk sets.

Materials

Paint: You can buy special lacquer for painting on glass. If you use acrylic paint, finish with a coat of clear lacquer.

Brushes: Use a ½" brush for the background color and a few art brushes for the designs.

Turpentine: Use for brush cleaning.

Container for paints: A foil cake plate will do.

Directions

Start with the easiest of designs—a flower-splashed vase.

1. Wash the glass thoroughly in a detergent to remove grease or dirt, rinse, and dry with a lint-free cloth.
2. Apply the background color with the ½" brush, working quickly to obtain an even surface. Allow to dry overnight.
3. For a good, solid background, apply a second coat and again let it dry overnight. After each painting, clean your brush with turpentine and then with soapy water.
4. To splash the flowers: Take your art brush with a lot of paint (not dripping) and dab on a little circle of dots. If you are using two colors, finish the circles of dots in one color first.

Have the petals near the top smaller and sparser than at the bottom. Now make your circles in the second color. In the center of each circle paint a dot in the contrasting color.

5. Again dry overnight. If you have used acrylic paint give your vase a coat of lacquer. When the lacquer has dried, set all the paints by putting the vase in a cold oven. Set the temperature for 250 degrees and after 5 minutes shut off the oven. Let the vase cool down in the oven.

Note: If you want to draw your own designs, use a chinograph pencil from an art supply store. If you prefer geometric designs, use masking tape for straight edges. If you want a three-dimensional effect, swish the paint around in the inside of the bottle and paint the design on the clear outside glass. And if you already know stenciling, use your designs for beautiful glass painting.

Initial Cost

From craft or paint shop: Glass paint, (4 primary colors) 50¢ each; brushes (art) 2 for about $2; brush (½″), 20¢; turpentine, 89¢.

DECOUPAGE AND COLLAGE

If you have ever held a scissors in your hand, collage or decoupage is for you. You can make anything from a simple dish to a framed work of art—lovely objects that will add hours of pleasure and extra dollars to your life!

Let us start by defining these two often-confused French words: decoupage and collage.

Decoupage is the art of decorating a surface with paper cutouts, for example, decorating a box with flowers cut out from a magazine. *Collage* is the art of pasting unrelated items on a surface. An example of that would be a picture of a girl surrounded by pressed flowers, a hair ribbon, a lace doily, aluminum foil, and the like, arranged artistically on a plain background.

Decoupage

A pretty dish like this one is easy to make and easy to sell!

Materials

A plain glass dish with a flat bottom; small scissors with round blades (manicure scissors); white paint (oil- or water-based); a 2" brush; a can of plastic spray; white glue; a small brush; and felt (cut to fit the bottom of the dish).

Directions

1. Using the manicure scissors, carefully cut out the flowers or scenes you have selected from magazines or prints. Seal the prints by spraying with the plastic. With the small brush, apply the glue to the front surface of the print and press it into place on the underside of the dish. Press with your fingers to remove any excess glue and wrinkles in the print. Remove excess glue with a damp sponge.
2. After a few hours, spray again with the sealer over the entire bottom.
3. When dry, paint the entire bottom of the dish with the white paint, once or twice as needed.
4. After the paint has dried, apply the glue to the bottom of the dish with a small brush. Then press the felt, cut to fit, over the glued surface.

Note: Because the upper surface is glass, you can make a 4" dish to hold a wine bottle, a 6" dish to use on a dressing table, and any size dish for an ash tray.

Haunt glass departments for ideas, and shop in bargain stores for inexpensive glassware. If you want to learn more about decoupage, your local library probably has many helpful books on this old craft.

Collage

Do not be intimidated by the words "work of art." Your creativity and taste could well outclass the average item sold in art galleries today. With collage, your finished work is influenced by how you feel about the objects you use, rather than by any formal art training.

If you sketch or paint, you can combine that training with collage. If you don't, you can trace and glue on and develop your own style.

Materials and Directions

You will need a backing board. Start with cardboard with even edges. A perfect backing board is Gesso, but until you have done your first collage, don't spend the money to buy it. The cardboard, however, must be stiff enough not to buckle under the weight of the paint and the objects you paste on it. Paint your backing board with any paint you may have in the house. If you use acrylic paint, make sure that it is smooth and thin—no lumps. This is the priming coat (as you oil painters know), and can be white or any background color according to your picture theme.

Suggestions

You may, instead of priming, cover your backing board with an interesting wrapping paper—shiny, black, or mirrored. You may decide to do a primitive with flowers and flower pots in bright colors—or a modern collage with stark white on black—or a portrait surrounded by paper lace, sequins, butterflies, bows, wallpaper flowers, or dried flowers.

Get yourself a collecting box. Put into it anything that could be used in a collage; use greeting cards to cut out as decoupage with your collage. A leaf, colored papers, bits of ribbon—the possibilities are endless!

Ask about clay paper at your craft or art store. If you ever want to combine a sketch with your collage, do it on clay paper, then cut it out and paste it on the backing board.

A beautiful gift is a birthday or family collage. With a photograph as a theme, you can decoupage a frame around it and then scramble around it anything related to birthdays and the family.

When the collage is done, fasten a hanging ring on the back of the board or frame it if you wish.

If friends and family like the collage, take it to a gift shop and let the owners know that you would like to take orders for birthday and family anniversary gifts. All you need to make up these personalized collages and decoupages is the snapshot from the customer.

If you plan to sell your decoupage or collage, try to develop a fashionable style—such as a primitive, elaborate Victorian, or pop art look. There will always be a buyer for your work of art.

Framing

You can frame your collage artistically, yet inexpensively, by upholstering a cheap or used frame with a fabric matching the collage. And it will be a custom look that will enhance your collage.

Plan your backboard and the frame to fit, then use material (patterned or plain) somewhere in the collage and on the frame. The result will be sensational!

Directions

1. Remove the glass and lay the frame face down on the cloth. Cut around the frame, leaving a margin of about 3 inches.
2. Spread newspaper on your work table and place the frame, right side up, on the paper. With the brush, spread glue on the face side of the frame.
3. Turn the frame over and center it down on the fabric with the margin even. Press down firmly, and let the glue dry partially.
4. With your brush, apply the glue to the outer and inner edges of the frame. Turn one side of the fabric over that side of the frame, pressing the fabric firmly along the outer and inner part of the frame. When you reach the corner, fold the material as if you were tucking in a sheet.
5. Continue around the frame until the material is entirely glued on. After the glue is thoroughly dry, cut away the excess fabric.
6. With a razor blade, remove the fabric inside the frame, leaving a margin of a few inches. The fabric you have cut out can be used within the collage.

7. Again with your razor blade, make a diagonal cut from the corners of the frame to the edges of the material. Then lift the material up and over the back of the frame. Before placing the fabric, brush it with glue. Press and smooth it firmly over the back of the frame. When it's dry, cut away the excess and re-place the glass.

SEASHELL CRAFTS

Seashell collecting is a centuries-old hobby. Around the world, art objects made from seashells include decorated stone walls, elaborate mosaics and nineteenth-century valentines.

If you are fortunate enough to live around the beach your collection, no doubt, has already started. Should you have friends living near the beach, ask them to collect shells for you. Since most people in the country do not live around any seashore, there are mail-order houses, hobby shops, and craft shops that will sell you the shells that you want. You can buy a mixture of many different kinds of shells or specimen shells for a particular project that you have in mind.

Discover this exciting world of shellcrafting. If you train yourself and learn every facet of this craft, you will be able to participate in the art fairs and craft shows and make money as well!

How to Begin

Start small with a purchase of one or two mixed bulk bags of shells. This will give you enough for a while. You will always be able to substitute one shell for another if you run short. If you are making a design pattern, know how many shells you will need at the beginning.

Shells should be washed and oiled when you bring them home because when they dry they become quite dull. Use a mixture of baby oil (or vegetable oil) and lighter fluid. *Caution*: Do this only outdoors. Make sure to avoid open flames as this mixture is extremely flammable. One part of oil to three parts of fluid is good for most shells. Place the shells in a large jar and swish around gently. Leave them in the solution for about three hours and then use a small strainer to take them out of the jar. Spread the shells

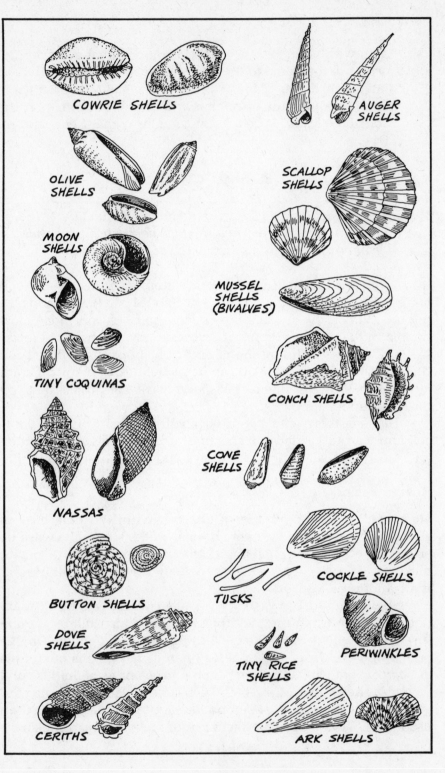

COWRIE SHELLS

AUGER SHELLS

OLIVE SHELLS

SCALLOP SHELLS

MOON SHELLS

MUSSEL SHELLS (BIVALVES)

TINY COQUINAS

CONCH SHELLS

CONE SHELLS

NASSAS

COCKLE SHELLS

BUTTON SHELLS

TUSKS

DOVE SHELLS

PERIWINKLES

TINY RICE SHELLS

CERITHS

ARK SHELLS

on newspapers to dry. If there is any oil left on the shells when you pick them up, use paper towels to blot them again.

Some of the more adaptable shells for projects from the hundreds of species are shown in the illustration on page 44.

Materials

The first materials that you need are sobo glue, bond cement, rubber cement, tweezers, pipe cleaners, soft brushes for cleaning, glass containers for keeping the shells sorted, a work board, and a couple of old pie tins for drying freshly glued shells. Pieces of driftwood are great for bases. If you make necklaces you will also need a small drill and nylon bead thread.

If you wish the shells to be a certain color, apply watercolor and wipe off before it dries. This will give a natural-looking stain.

Necklaces

Have you ever found a Mexican sand dollar? If you have, handle it gently and coat it with several coats of shellac. When it's dry, put a leather thong through the top of it for a great summertime necklace. If you don't have any leather, colored yarn will do nicely.

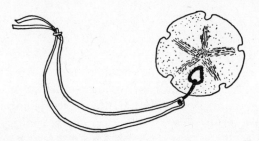

Mussel shells, small beads, or tiny shells (pierced with a needle) can be strung on heavy nylon thread to make a dramatic necklace.

To make an olive shell and colored glass bead necklace, drill through olive shells and string on jeweler's wire, alternating with the beads. The olive shells can be first bleached and then lightly stained with watercolor.

With strong nylon thread (or fishing line), many different shells can be used. You can mix almost all types of shells and arrange them with seeds, coral, wooden and glass beads, or anything else that strikes your imagination.

SHELL-DECORATED MIRRORS

Easy to make and easy to sell!

Materials

One 10″ round frame, one 8″ round frame, thin plywood backing, sobo glue, rubber cement, shell cement, olive shells, clam shells, moon or snail shells.

Directions

First select the shells you are going to use. Remove the mirror from the frame, and clean the frame of any dust or old glue. Arrange the shells in a pattern. Try different varieties and combinations. When you use a large shell, you will need smaller shells to fill in the gaps.

Sobo glue dries slowly and is water-soluble. It will hold on wood frames or glass, but it will not hold on slick surfaces. Keep a wet towel handy to clean off your fingers. When you are using a shell that has an aperture, simply fill it with glue-soaked cotton first.

SANDCASTING

With sand and driftwood, you can make a work of art for souvenir and gift shops. A seabird, standing on a piece of driftwood, is easy to make in a simple mold. So is a dove or quail!

Materials

A wire strainer, a plastic measuring cup, a ½-gallon plastic pail, plaster of paris, two 8″ rods (from hardware store), driftwood or a square of cork for the base.

Directions

If you do not work right on the beach, you will need a large pan, deep enough to mold the sand for a bird 10″ long, 6″ deep, and 8″ wide (including the legs). A large plastic pan is excellent because any plaster of paris hardened on it can easily be bent off.

To prepare the sand for casting, clean it by sifting the sand through the strainer into the casting pan. Mix enough water with the strained sand so that it is just damp. The sand is ready when you can stick your finger ⌐ .o it and make a firm hole. The sand must be firmly packed and level.

Before you begin to scoop out your bird, you may want to draw it out on paper for the proportions. Scoop out the body to shape. Put in the face, beak, and wings. Lay the wire legs where they should be, about 2″ above the bottom of the body. Press the legs firmly 2″ into the sand (making sure they are straight). The 2 inches showing in the mold of the body will be covered by the plaster of paris.

To prepare the plaster of paris, put 3 cups of water into the pail. Add 1 cup of plaster, stirring with a stick until it has a rich, creamy consistency. Immediately before it begins to harden, pour the plaster into the top of the mold. Let the plaster harden for at least one hour.

If you can still scratch the plaster easily with your fingernail, it is too soft. When it's hard, dig the sand away from the edges of the mold. Work a hand under the mold on each side and gently lift it.

With an old brush, whisk away the surplus sand. Your sand sculpture will always have that soft sandy surface. The legs can be glued into holes in a piece of driftwood or a firm square of cork. You can even cast a square of plaster, holding the bird as the plaster hardens.

Sand Casting Candles

Candle casting is done exactly as previously described, except that you pour wax into the mold instead of plaster.

Small Gelatine Mold

When the sifted sand is just damp enough, press any round object (even a rubber ball will do) firmly into the sand about halfway. At the bottom of the mold, press your finger into the sand evenly four times for the legs.

To prepare the paraffin (supermarket or craft shop), melt it slowly in a saucepan on low heat for about ten minutes, along with any colored crayon. If you have stubs of leftover candles, press one firmly in the center of the mold and pour out the hot paraffin to the top of the mold below the wick.

If you have no leftover candle stubs, use a wick (from a craftshop, 7¢ per yard). Dip the wick into the hot wax, stretching it taut as it hardens. Poke it into the center of the mold, and hold it straight as you pour the paraffin into the mold. Trim the wick to the proper length.

For pretty candle shapes, any small pudding or gelatin mold can be used to press your sandcrafted candle.

Plaster casting and wax casting are both stimulating. As you walk along the beach, the shells, stones and driftwood become inspirations for your imagination.

Plaster of paris is inexpensive—so is paraffin—and sandcasting is a craft that allows good profits for you!

HAND-SHAPED CANDLES

Hand-shaped candles are easy to make. The only tool you need is a spoon to make the popular taper candle that people buy for their dinner tables.

Materials

From your kitchen you need two saucepans, a spoon, a tall pitcher, and a cooking thermometer.

From a craft shop you need paraffin wax, stearin, powdered wax dye, wicks.

Directions

1. Start with a 9″ candle. You can obtain the correct size wick from a craft shop. Cut wick 4″ longer than the candle.
2. For a 9″ candle, put 5 cups of paraffin in a saucepan. Into the other saucepan, measure ½ parts stearin to 10 parts paraffin. Add the dye to the stearin. A pinch of powdered dye is enough for a pint of wax.
3. Slowly melt the paraffin over a low heat.
4. Slowly melt the stearin acid/dye mixture over a low heat.
5. Add the stearin dye to the paraffin and reheat to 180 degrees on the cooking thermometer. Never let it smoke.
6. Dip the wick into the liquid wax, leaving a few inches undipped for holding. For a half-minute, hold the wick taut until it is stiff.
7. Check the paraffin at 180 degrees, then remove it from the heat. Hold the wick over the pan, and spoon hot wax down the wick, while rotating the wick between your fingers. Between each pouring, allow the surface to cool. Keep the paraffin at 180 degrees while forming for a glossy finish. Then heat the paraffin to 200 degrees, spoon over the finished candle, and immediately dip it into a pitcher of cold water.
8. Trim the wick.

9. *Note:* If you prefer to dip rather than spoon the candle, you will need a metal jug (as tall as the candle you wish to make). Ask at your craft supply shop about melting/pouring containers. Remember to weight the wick so that it will remain taut while dipping.

Initial Costs

Paraffin (block or powdered) is available at craft shops for about $4 for a 5½″ block. *Hint:* Look for paraffin in the jelly-making department of supermarkets and discount stores for better prices. Your other costs will include 40¢ for 2 oz. of stearin, 50¢ for the dye, and 7¢ per yard for wicks.

Look at the prices of candles in shops. You will see that you now have a beautiful craft to make at a reasonable cost—and to sell for a very pleasing profit!

Safety Note

If you should splash a drop of hot paraffin on your skin, immediately run cold tap water over it. The paraffin will peel off. Continue running cold water over the skin for a few minutes.

BAYBERRY CANDLES

Sweet-smelling bayberry candles, the pride of the Colonial housewife! Not just for the holidays—but for any day you want to fill a room with fragrance. You can make them easily—to keep for yourself or to sell for extra dollars!

Materials

A 7-oz tuna fish can, a block of paraffin, stearic acid, blue color concentrate, candle wicking, bayberry essence, an eye dropper, scotch tape, cooking oil.

Note: Craft shops carry the paraffin (so do some supermarkets), the wicking, the stearic acid, and the color concentrate. The craft shop has or can obtain the essential bayberry oil.

Directions

1. Make a small hole in the bottom of the tuna can (be sure it's clean). Rub the inside with cooking oil. Melt a ½-pound block

of paraffin over a very low heat for about 10 minutes. When the wax is completely melted, add ½ teaspoon stearic acid (which slows the burning of the candle). Now add 1 teaspoon of the blue concentrate. Remove the wax from the heat and add 30 drops of the bayberry essence with a dropper.

2. Dip a 5″ piece of the wicking into the wax, pull straight, and let it harden. Insert the waxed end down through the can and the bottom hole, leaving ½ inch protruding. Fasten the end tightly with tape.

3. Hold the wick steady with one hand while you pour the hot wax into the can, to within ¼ inch of the top. When you pour, be sure that the wax is hot enough so it will not scum. Hold the wick between two skewers while pouring the wax. Wait about 3 hours for the wax to cool firmly, remove the tape, dip the can briefly in hot water, and shake out the candle.

4. If you prefer a shiny candle, polish it with an old nylon stocking dipped in vegetable oil. Clip off the bottom wick. Cut the top wick to the desired length.

6. A little decoration—sequins, artificial flowers, and so on— makes the bayberry candle a perfect gift shop item!

Note: Paraffin costs about $4 for a 5½-pound block. Comparison-shop your craft shops, and don't overlook supermarkets as a potential source for the best price.

HAND PRINTING ON FABRIC

Hand printing on fabric is a very old craft. The technique has been passed down from generation to generation. Those skilled in this craft have their artistic projects in shops and boutiques.

Directions

Before you begin hand printing on textiles, you may wonder how colorfast the colors are. The answer is that textile colors are fast if you use a setting agent and heat. If you do not use this "fixer," you can expect some fading.

If you are a beginner, start with the simplest method of hand printing—nature printing. It is done with a vegetable or fruit— such as a carrot, onion, or apple. After you cut the vegetable or fruit, let it sit on a newspaper for about a half hour to get the juices out.

Let us start with carrot printing. Cut a large firm carrot and dry it cut side down on a newspaper. Leave yourself about 2½" of the carrot as a handle. Next, draw a circle in the middle, and star points out to the edges. With a sharp knife, hollow out the carrot away from the design.

You can make your own designs on the carrot with a little practice. A half onion or half apple needs no cutting, as the rings of the onion and the core of the apple stamp out a beautiful design.

Fabric Colors

Start with a few premixed colors. These ready-mixed textile colors must be fixed. If you decide on a color lighter than the ready-made color you purchased, you can lighten it with an extender. Later on, when you have progressed to a more advanced hand printing, you can consult books from the library on procedures for mixing your own colors.

Placemats

Materials

The best material for color printing is muslin or poplin. If you have old plain sheets, cut them up to the size you want with enough room for hemming. If you use new poplin or muslin, the sizing must be washed out and the material carefully ironed, so that crease marks will not interfere with the printing.

Preparation

The printing table must have a smooth surface and be large enough for your materials. Cover it with a smooth ironing board pad or a woolen blanket. Stretch a clean piece of old sheet over it and tack it firmly on the underside with thumbtacks. You can use a heavy piece of plywood covered in the same way. Your working area should be at least 3' wide and 3' long.

To avoid any dripping, keep the color jars and the brushes on a small tray and cover the material that you are not printing on with clean paper. Keep a small piece of your material for testing the carrot stamp.

Directions

Find the center of the placemat by folding the placemat gently lengthwise and crosswise. Mark it with a dot. Use this center for the first printing, and work up and down from there. Do *not* use pencil guidelines; rather, use a ruler weighted down to keep it from moving. Any guidelines may be corrected in your fixing process later.

Pin the placemat on the printing board with a pin at each corner and in the middle of the sides. Brush the color onto the carrot stamp. Press the stamp down on the material, but avoid any excess color that may drip off your pattern.

You can stamp in rows or in random patterns. You can even stamp edges over edges for a soft effect.

Heat Setting

Twenty hours after the printing, begin your heat setting to fix the colors. Heat setting does *not* change the color.

To bake the printed material in the oven, smooth the fabric on the table over tissue paper or a clean cloth. At one end, fold the cloth or tissue paper over the printed fabric, then roll the fabric and paper loosely together. It is important to roll loosely so that the temperature can reach the inside layers evenly. Again, roll an extra piece of cloth or paper around the roll, leaving the ends loose.

Heat an electric oven to 250 degrees. Place the roll on a clean baking tray, and remove after 10 minutes. If you have a gas-oven, heat it to 350 degrees, turn off the oven, and put in the roll. If you don't have a thermostat on your oven, or if it does not operate efficiently, use an oven thermometer.

Among the items that lend themselves to nature printing are bookmarks, napkins, doilies, placemats, plain cloth shopping bags, paper-covered boxes, and plain rolls of paper printed for gift wrapping. If you find yourself looking for more creative and advanced hand printing, you can refer to guidebooks in the library.

If you go on to block stamping, buy your standard block (linoleum mounted on wood). Linoleum is easy to cut, so you can design and cut your stamp. You may even make your own stamps in nonstandard sizes.

Because nature printing and block printing are different in technique and instruments, we suggest only the possibilities of this ancient art. There are many books in your library to teach and insipire you.

WEAVING

Today, we do not need to weave material by hand. There will, however, always be creative people who enjoy working their looms and selling hand-loomed articles to appreciative buyers.

For those who have always wanted to loom, but have never done so for lack of time, here is a little history of weaving—a history that gives us an appreciation of the marvelous yarns available today.

Weaving began with the conquest of raw material—grasses, palm leaves, and string had to be prepared for weaving baskets and mats. The first usable thread was discovered from the twisting of the curly wool of sheep, when the spinner and the spindle were used. Later, the fibers from the silkworm were spun into thread for garment fabrics. Wool, linen, cotton, and silk all had to be converted before weaving could begin.

Weaving can be a simple art or it can be a complex art. Children can be taught to weave small objects with warp ends fastened to a beginner loom, or fastened outdoors to a tree, or fastened indoors to a bedpost. If you have already been weaving as a leisure hobby, you can now progress to a practical and profitable occupation. If you are just beginning, you can quickly learn a few fascinating steps until you are weaving beautiful objects to sell.

Because it is beyond the scope of this book to teach weaving, read through the following outline pages. Your nearby high schools and colleges may have arts and crafts workshops. Obtain from your library a few of the suggested books. Talk to the owner of a weaving shop.

Today, walk into any weaving shop and see the fantastic assortment of yarns and the gorgeous colors for shawls, capes, blankets, rugs, and placemats!

The Loom

The history of the loom is also complex, and you can read in your library books the evolution of the loom in different countries and different cultures. Since you, the beginner, can now consider weaving as a joy, and a means of making extra money, let us look at the simplest explanation of the loom: It weaves together the *warp* (the lengthwise thread) and the *weft* (the crosswise thread).

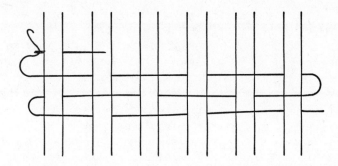

The loom is a cloth-weaving instrument, and it can range from a simple wooden frame to a factory-powered machine. The home weaver, however, needs only a small table loom to begin with. The table loom can be only 8 inches large, but the medium size, a 20-inch size, is quite large and practical. Looms are made in several different styles, including a folding model.

Weaving and looming has a vocabulary all its own, and after you have your loom and instructions on its use, you will recognize the following terms:

Warp Beam: At the back of the loom on which the warp or lengthwise thread is wound.

Warp Lifting Shafts: The warp thread is threaded through the two shafts, even numbers in one, odd numbers in the other. When one is lifted, it creates a shed through which the weft is passed. The next time the other shaft is lifted; the alternating movement places the weave over and under the warp.

Heddles:	The eyes or loops on the shafts, through which the lengthwise thread is drawn with a hook.
Shuttles:	For small booms, the flat shuttle is wound with the crosswise yarn, and thrown (a weaver's word for passing) through the shed from side to side.
Lease Sticks:	Before threading the warp yarn through the heddle eye, the thread is spread with a pair of lease sticks. The length equals the width of the loom.
Beater:	A cross loom piece that pushes or beats the weft into place after it is passed through the shed of warp yarns.
Yarn:	Weaving yarns come in skeins, spools or cones. Each one is numbered by yarn count. This tells you how many yards of thread in a pound, so that quantity can be calculated exactly. *Note:* the size of the loom determines what you can weave. Example, an 18″ placemat would need a 20″ loom. A 40″ handwoven tweed would need a 40″ loom.

In Guatemala, young girls, squatting on the ground, weave their colorful primitives with a simple loom called a "girdle loom." One end is fastened by a rod in the ground, the weaver end is held by a loop over the body. Today, our looms are equally simple to use—it is the beautiful yarns and colors that transform the simplest weave into a thing of beauty.

Consider the saleability of the following weavings:

Table mats:	Rough grey yarn, with shimmering aluminum interwoven threads of soft wool. Stiff linen and grass in dark and light color values.
Cushions:	Sharp black and white simple weaves.
Bedspreads:	Stripes sewn together in light, medium and dark green progression.

Here are some additional sources for more information on weaving: *Handweaver and Craftsman Magazine*, 220 Fifth Avenue, New York, N.Y. 10001. (A must for weavers. Information on techniques, new books, exhibits, yarns, tools, sources of material. Look up back issues in your library.)

Some books on weaving include: *Weaving is Fun* by Jean Wilson, published by Van Nostrand Reinhold. (A guide for beginning weavers.) *The Techniques of Rug Weaving* by Peter Collingwood, published by Watson-Guptil. *The Art of Weaving* by Else Regensteiner, published by Van Nostrand Reinhold. (A handbook for every weaver, beginner and expert, offering complete coverage of the materials, equipment, techniques and creative possibilities of the medium.)

Also the Library of Congress in Washington, D.C. will send you free government pamphlets on weaving.

LEATHERWORK

Leatherwork is an ancient craft—and a fun project. Because synthetics will never replace leather in sheer beauty, you will have appreciative buyers of your art.

Start with a leather bookmark. It's simple to make and easy to sell. You can follow these step-by-step instructions with an eye toward extra income. A basketfull for a gift shop or bookstore to sell for you!

Materials

1. *A cutting board.* You probably have a bread board with a smooth, wooden surface. Even a thick piece of cardboard can be used, then thrown away when cut up.
2. *A cutting knife.* You can use a very sharp penknife or a single-edge razorblade (in a holder from the hardware store). But for serious work, you will need a special leather cutting knife from a hobby shop or craft shop (about $1).
3. *Pattern material.* This can be cardboard or strong paper.
4. *Leather.*

Types of Leather

You can find the leather in any craft shop, hobby shop or leatherwork shop.

You have the choice of:

1. *Sheepskin*—cheap, soft and easy to handle. It comes in a variety of colors and finishes.
2. *Goatskin*—smooth, supple, soft-textured and attractive. It is more expensive than sheepskin.
3. *Pigskin*—attractive and naturally pierced through by tiny holes in sets of three. Also more expensive than sheepskin or goatskin.
4. *Suede*—the leather with a rough, or napped, surface. It is finished by buffing the skin until it is as soft as velvet. Excellent for bookmarks.
5. *Hide*—a thick leather made from cowhide. Too thick for work with small articles, but the split hide, made by dividing the hide into thin layers, can be used for your bookmarks.

When you are starting, ask the supplier if he or she has a small parcel of leather remnants. There should be several pieces large enough for bookmarks, and the price should be low. When you are sure of your leatherwork, you can branch out to split cowhide (the cheapest at about $1 a square foot) or to exotic reptile skins.

Your Pattern

Always make a pattern, for even the simplest items. It cuts waste to a minimum. For the first bookmark, you can use a paper pattern; later, for more than one cutting, you can use thick cardboard.

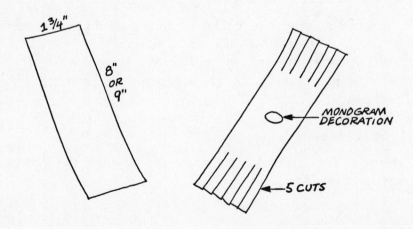

Transcribing the Pattern

Use a metal straightedge ruler to guide your knife (do not use a plain wooden ruler). As a matter of fact, any straight edge piece of metal can be used. Keep the knife at right angles to the leather to avoid a slanted edge. Never use scissors—because this crushes the fibers, and you will have a fuzzy edge.

After cutting out the main shape of the bookmark, mark out the slits at the edges with a pencil, use the ruler and cut. You will have an attractive and balanced bookmark.

Decoration

You can design some decoration that you like (such as monograms, flowers, leaves, mottos), trace one, or buy an applique at a fabric store. Consult the experts at the craft shops.

How to Decorate with Leather

There are two ways to decorate leather, *applying* and *modeling*.

1. Applying: After you have cut the pattern for your decoration, place it on a thick piece of contrasting-color leather. Cut it out and glue it to the bookmark. After glueing, always press the bookmark between two boards, with a weight on top, until it is dry.
2. Modeling: This is interesting to do, and you will have the effect of the leather being carved.
    a. Use a hard, waterproof surface, such as marble, plateglass or formica.
    b. Dampen the skin thoroughly, and keep it damp with a pressed-out sponge the entire time you are working on it.
    c. Place a sheet of carbon paper, carbon side up, on your working surface. Place the bookmark, wrong side down, on the carbon. Place the pattern of your ornament on the right side of the bookmark, and draw around it with a sharp instrument (only to *impress*, not cut). Remove the pattern and make the outline deeper by going around it two or three times with a sharp instrument. When you turn over the bookmark, you should have a carbon imprint to help you work. You now press out, from the reverse side, the pattern within the carbon outline. You can

buy a special modeling tool for this, but you will find tools in your kitchen—such as the end of a small spoon. When you have pressed out the pattern on the wrong side, turn it over and depress the background around the outline.

3. Modeling is done by alternating the pressing out the ornament from the back, and depressing the background from the right side. Remember, always keep the leather damp while you are working on it.

Once you have made this beautiful, genuine leather bookmark, you can fill that basket of "Gifts Under $5" for your book shop, craft shop, or gift shop!

If your leatherworking becomes your money-making project, you may then wish to make purses, tote bags, bookcovers, and the like. You can find advanced instruction for any of these saleable items at your local library.

PAPERMAKING USING JUNK MAIL

There has been a popular return of papermaking services, and you can make many types of beautiful paper right in your kitchen!

Translucent papers for special occasion cards, arty-looking papers with fibers or rose leaves blended into different designs, papers of different colors, papers for greeting cards—all this and more can be made from the junk mail that you receive and common things around the house or out in the garden (even weeds!).

These things include lint from your dryer (cotton only), dried rose petals, green grass, mushrooms (dried or fresh), iris leaves, thistle, banana peels (cooked), and anything else that looks interesting enough to add to the paper in the blender.

There is a large market for original, handmade papers, so get out your blender, clear the kitchen table, and let's go to work!

Materials

1. Junk mail
2. Baking pan
3. Pelon (from fabric store)
4. Two wooden frames

5. Large dishpan
6. 8" × 10" aluminum screen
7. 8" × 10" piece of polyester organdy (silkscreen)
8. Blender
9. 18" × 24" sheet of glass or plexiglass
10. Nails
11. Sponges
12. Large water pitcher and some water

Directions

1. Make your aluminum frame by nailing the piece of screen onto a wooden frame.
2. Make the silkscreen the same way, by nailing the organdy to the second frame.
3. Clear off your kitchen table and keep a mop handy, as this is a very wet project.
4. Tear some junk mail or newspapers into pieces the size of nickels. A cup of this blend is about the right amount for your first batch.
5. Fill the blender almost to the top with water.
6. Turn on the blender to its slowest speed to get the paper moving around, then alternate the speeds from slow to fast every five seconds until the paper begins to look like pulp.
7. Pour this mixture into a large dishpan, and add about ten more batches from your blender. When you are selecting the junk mail to tear up for the pulp, select colors that you like if you have a special project in mind. For instance, if you use dried mushrooms with mostly white papers in a batch, your finished paper will be a medium brown. Using grass in the blender will turn the paper a light green.
8. Cut the pelon into 12" × 15" squares, and lay it flat on the glass. (The pelon acts as a blotter.)
9. Pick up the box with the aluminum screen right side up, (screen on the bottom), and slowly slide the frame into the pulp, scooping up the pulp as you lift it out of the water. If there are any bare spots, repeat this process until you have a nice even coat of pulp on top of the screen.
10. Gently blot off the excess water with a sponge, turn the screen upside down on the pelon (just like an upside-down

cake), and lift the screen slowly off the pulp. The paper will cling to the pelon to dry.

11.   When the paper is completely dry, pick up the finished paper carefully by peeling it around the edges first. Lift it slowly and place it between clean sheets of paper.

12.   The silkscreen is used by turning the screen upside down, so that the organdy is the bottom of the screen and the wooden frame is the top. Holding the screen in this manner, scoop the pulpy water into it.

13.   Place the pelon in your baking pan because the silkscreen method is a little wetter, and turn the silkscreen upside down onto the pelon. The paper will come right off the screen. Blot it carefully and let it dry.

Using this method, you will be able to make a thicker paper, and you can use the fibers, straw, or whatever for a more interesting design.

Using junk mail is fun, because it comes in so many colors. When you want something more interesting, start mixing rose leaves, grass, or anything else you want to experiment with. Try the mushrooms—elegant when used with white cotton lint from your dryer.

Advertise your talents in papermaking. Take your samples around the neighborhood and to gift shops and boutiques. You will be delighted at the reaction.

CUSTOM PARTY FAVORS FOR CHILDREN

At birthday time, parents buy favors for little party guests to take home. You can make favors to sell to parents in your neighborhood, saving them money, and make dollars for yourself! Using cork and wood, the following four party favors can be made inexpensively to sell in your neighborhood or to your nearby party store.

Gingerbread Man (for children aged one to three)

Materials and Costs

Cork sheet ⅛" thick (two ⅛" × 12" × 36" thick sheets will go a long way); gold or silver cord; sequins; glue; white poster paint; a nail. These can all be purchased at a crafts store. Cork sheets cost about

$1.60 per package; the cord is 10¢ to 20¢ a yard; sequins are about 50¢ per package.

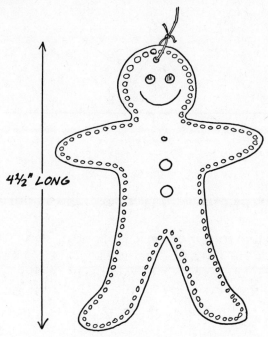

4½" LONG

Directions

1. Draw or trace your gingerbread man on stiff paper and cut it out to use as a pattern. Outline the gingerbread man on the cork sheeting and cut it out with scissors.
2. "Frost" the gingerbread man with the paint, as you would a real cookie. Punch a hole at the top with a clean nail. Paste the sequins on the eyes, and coat the buttons with sequins. Draw a smiling mouth. Thread gold or silver cord through the hole and knot.

Tell parents that the children can hang their gingerbread men on a Christmas tree or window shade cord. If you wish to make this favor into a gift tag, simply glue white paper on the back.

Cute Cork Puppy (for children aged three to five)

Materials

One 2" long bottle cork; one 1" long bottle cork; a brown felt-tipped pen; a darning needle; different-colored round toothpicks. You will find corks in a hardware store, the pen in a stationery store, the toothpicks in a supermarket.

Directions

1. Using the pen, paint the eyes, nose, and mouth on the smaller cork.
2. Cut the toothpicks for the legs about 1¼" long. The tail should be about 1½" long. Cut toothpick for the neck about ¾" long. Using the large cork for the body, start the holes for the toothpicks with the darning needle, and put the puppy together.
3. Use the pen to color the puppy in patches like a beagle's.

Party Sippers (for children aged three and up)

Materials

Purchase these items at your craft store: plastic sippers; cork balls 1¼" wide; cork sheet ¹⁄₁₆" thick; small fluffy feathers; poster paint; sequins; darning needle.

Directions

1. Through the center of the cork ball, make a hole the same size as the plastic straw.
2. Cut two little wings from the cork sheet, and glue them to the cork ball.
3. Push in the round ends of the toothpick for the beak.
4. Paint the bird a pretty color with the poster paint. When dry, paint the eyes.
5. To make the tail, push the darning needle into the ball, and then insert a feather in the hole.
6. Push the plastic sipper in place and tie a small, bright ribbon under the bird's head, to keep the sipper from slipping.

Party Pencil Favorites (for children aged five and up)

Materials

Cork balls 1¼" wide; bright strands of knitting yarn; glue; black felt-tipped pen; new pencils.

Directions

1. Make a hole in the cork to push the pencil into.
2. Cut a few strands of the knitting yarn into twelve 4" pieces.
3. Glue the strands to the top of the head for hair.

4. Leave the cork natural, but paint the eyes, nose, and mouth with the felt-tipped pen.

If you want to make the hat, slice a ¼" piece off the wide end of a 1¼" bottle cork, and then glue it to a 1" high piece of cork. Attach the hat by pushing a toothpick through the hat and the head. Push the pencil into the smiling head.

Note: When you make these inexpensive favors, keep an accurate record of your customer purchases. They you can set a reasonable price for the party shop or customer—and make yourself a nice profit!

4

WALLPAPERING—WHO, ME?

Sure you! Wallpapering is great for the waistline, and it's a way to meet new people. Start this new profession by yourself or get a friend to share the work and money with you.

If you are only going to be a paper-hanger, you needn't worry about choosing patterns; your customers will give you the paper they want you to hang. But you may want to save some money by papering your own home, or you may be asked for your opinion on wallpapering your client's home; for this reason we include some basic information about wallpaper here.

The right pattern in the wrong room can be disastrous, so let's talk about the different types of papers before we get into the technique of actually hanging the paper.

Machine-printed papers and custom-print papers are usually 27 inches wide and 15 feet long. Each roll normally contains 30 square feet. The size of the pattern determines how much of the roll is usable. This is called the *repeat pattern*, and it is always printed on the front of each roll. Most wallpaper is cut into double rolls; a pattern with a 20-inch repeat wouldn't match the adjoining strip many times before you would run out of a single roll.

A wallpaper pattern may look very attractive in the store but be all wrong for the room you want to hang it in. For this reason you should borrow samples from the store and look at the pattern at home.

TYPES OF WALL COVERINGS

Vinyl Wall Coverings

Vinyl wall coverings are divided into two categories: paper-backed and canvas-backed. Vinyl is a great paper to use in bathrooms, kitchens, hallways, laundry rooms, and nurseries. These are the rooms that always get touched by hands and need to be cleaned more often.

The advantages of this paper are obvious—it is not delicate and can be easily washed down with a damp cloth. The vinyl background can be shiny or have a dull matte finish, can be any color, and sometimes is even textured. Vinyls can also be made to resemble something else. They are tough and flexible, easy to hang, and can look like grass, cloth, cork, linen, silk, or suede. Vinyl is not expensive and is in great demand because of its durability and ease of handling.

Flocks and Foil Papers

Flocks and foils are elegant papers. They are harder to hang and stiffer to handle, but the effect is great and exciting. After you are able to handle these custom-looking wallpapers, you can charge more per roll to hang.

Flocked wallpapers have a fuzzy raised pattern, which is glued to the background. Most flocked wallpapers have traditional patterns, which are wonderful with antique furniture. Most of the designs resemble contemporary printed velvets or roses. Flocked wallpapers have been around for years and were originally made to look like upholstery.

Foil papers are relatively new. Many of the patterns resemble leaf designs in gold or silver, but they can be any color or texture. The effects of this paper can be incredibly striking and will add light in any room. *Note:* Your walls must be perfectly smooth before your foils are applied, or every imperfection in the walls will show through when the paper dries.

Scenic Murals and Graphics

Scenic murals and graphics have very special functions. Murals are printed in a series of sheets that are hung together to create a scene. They are usually used for only one wall in a room. Murals depict forest scenes, seascapes, animals for children's rooms, ships, and many other themes.

Murals are found in most wallpaper stores and are relatively easy to hang. A mural for a dark room without a window can work wonders.

Graphics come in many designs also. Some are very dramatic and contemporary and will perk up an uninteresting entry. If you want an exciting entry, try this in the living room.

Woven Wall Coverings

Woven wall coverings are one of the most popular papers. They are always paper-backed and need care in installation to prevent the weave from pulling away from its backing. This paper is not for the beginner, but if you can get some professional help with this versatile paper on how to size the walls and handle adhesives, you and your clients will be thrilled with the results.

Silk on paper-backing is also luxurious, delicate, and expensive. Linens in all weaves, colors, and textures can create the most subtle and understated of backgrounds. A natural linen wall covering has a fibrous texture that resembles rope, and it is very effective in any hallway. It will also highlight any room that needs a feeling of space and light.

Choosing the Wallpaper

It is difficult to know what you want until you study the effect that you are trying to achieve. Wallpaper stores will let you check out their books to take home with you.

Since a lot of the patterns also have matching fabrics, a great many variations of plans are possible. Wallpaper coverings can have a diverse effect on a room. They can provide a subtle background or a startling pattern that dominates the room. *Always* let the function of the room dictate the kind of wallpaper used.

At first, try to stay away from difficult papers. Prepasted papers seem to be made for beginners, and you can do a terrific job with a little practice. Don't wallpaper a ceiling unless you have professional help with you. Small patterns on a white background are delightful in a small bedroom, children's room, or bathroom. Coordinate the wallpaper with the color of the rug.

Stop and think about the room you are doing. Is the room too light or too dark? Does the ceiling bother you because it looks too high or too low? Do you get a cold feeling when you walk into the room?

All of these feelings can be corrected by carefully choosing the patterns and colors of your wallpaper. Remember:

1. Papers with dark backgrounds tend to make a room look smaller.
2. Vertical designs can make a low ceiling appear higher.
3. Horizontal designs can make a narrow room look wider.
4. Reds, oranges, and yellows are warm colors. Greens and blues are cool colors. Consider the "temperature" of a color before you choose.
5. Papers with solid colors or plain textures are the easiest to hang.
6. Measure accurately, carefully butt the seams, and don't stretch the paper during hanging.

How to Order Wallpaper

A single roll of wallpaper contains 36 square feet. About 6 square feet are lost in matching the patterns (this varies, depending on the pattern). First measure the room in feet. Then measure the height of the ceiling. Multiply the room measurement by the ceiling height for the square feet. Since you have about 30 square feet in a single roll, simply divide this number by 30 and you will get the total number of single rolls you will need. Deduct one single roll for every two openings (door or windows).

If you are still not sure, order an extra roll. You can return it for a refund if you don't use it.

Where to Start

The very best place to start the first strip of paper is the back of the door, because you will avoid any future problems in a prominent area. Measure the width of the wallpaper, subtract an inch, and place a mark to the right of the opening. Take the chalked plumb line (colored chalk), and tack it close to the ceiling over the mark.

Hold the line taut and snap it. Your first strip will be hung to the left of this line, and all of the remaining strips will be hung to the right of your first strip.

Cutting the Roll to Match the Pattern

It's wonderful to have a nice, long table, but you can measure just as well on the floor. Mark off on the floor the exact height of the ceiling, and add 3 inches to the top and bottom of your *first strip*. Match the pattern to the second strip before you cut it.

You always need the previous strip to match the pattern for your next strip. As each strip is cut, mark the pattern on the back of the paper, and reroll each cut strip so that the face of the paper (pattern) is always on the inside.

For easy handling when you are ready to hang the paper, always roll the paper starting at the bottom of the roll and end it at the top.

Hanging the Paper

Fill the water tray a little more than halfway with clean lukewarm water, and put the rerolled paper in the water for about a minute. You can apply the paper to the wall directly from the water tray.

Take the top of the strip, stand on a ladder, and unroll the paper very carefully, moving up the ladder at the same time. The first strip *must* line up with your plumb line. Place the strip at the top of the wall next to the ceiling, leaving about 3 inches overlapping the ceiling.

Line up the edge of the paper with the chalk mark, and give the paper a light overall brushing with your smoothing brush. This will hold the paper in place.

If you need to straighten the paper, use the palms of your hands to slide the paper into place. After you have the paper in position, smooth it out for air bubbles, and go over it again with the smoothing brush. Stroke out from the middle, and up and down from the middle.

The next strip goes on in the same way, lining it up for a perfect match of patterns, butting the edges as tight and close as you can. It is most important that you do not stretch the paper while straightening up your edges, because this will cause the paper to shrink back when it dries. Corners will fit better if you measure the distance your paper will go on the next wall, and mark it with a plumb line. Place the plumb line about 2 inches away from where the edge will be, and line it up. Use the back of the smoothing brush to firm the paper into the corners. Use your hands to smooth out the paper.

When the paper dries a little, trim off the surplus paper at the top and bottom of each strip. Buy plenty of razors, because they dull very fast. Use sponges frequently to wipe off the excess paste from the edges. Save leftover paper; it will come in handy to cover your switchplates, a nice decorator touch.

PREPASTED WALLPAPER:
THE NUMBER ONE CHOICE FOR BEGINNERS

There have been tremendous improvements in prepasted wallpapers over the last several years. Surface coatings are better, so that wallpaper may be used on walls and ceilings in any area of your home. Paper stocks, factory trimmings, the paste system, and packaging are improved, which permit faster, easier hanging. Prepasted wallpaper is pasted at the factory with the proper type of adhesive.

No mixing or applying paste is necessary. All you do is soak the strip in water before hanging. Following are *complete* hanging instructions for prepasted wallpaper. If you can read these instructions before you start and as you are working, the finished job will be a professional one.

Tools of the Trade

If you are going to paper one or two walls, purchase an inexpensive wallpaper kit. This kit and a pair of scissors are about all you need to buy. If you plan to wallpaper professionally, here is the list of materials that you need:

putty knife	sandpaper	water tray
trimming knife	scissors	plumb line and chalk
smoothing brush	plastic pail	razor blades
step ladder	screwdriver	spackling paste
seam roller	straightedge	wall sizing
large sponge	marking pencil	

REMOVING OLD PAPER

In general, old wallpaper should be removed to avoid future problems, but if your heart (and back) isn't up to all that work, and you want to know if you can get away without paper removal, the old paper *must* meet these requirements: There can be no more than one or two layers of old paper. Old paper should adhere tightly everywhere. Rough spots should be smoothed with sandpaper. If the old paper is strippable, remove it. If the paper is foil, remove it. Rub the old paper with a damp cloth and if the old pattern comes off, remove the paper. *Note*: Wallpaper removers are available and can be rented.

GENERAL PREPARATION

Wash all walls with soap and water. Rinse thoroughly with plain water. Bathroom or kitchen walls with high-gloss paint should be sanded lightly, or use a wall covering adhesive that you can brush on. Let this dry before you hang the paper. Any uneven wall area must be made smooth. Gouges, cracks, and nail holes should be filled with spackling paste and sanded smooth when dry.

If you wish to paper over a door or other painted surface, sand lightly and then wash with soap and water.

New plaster and new plasterboard must cure (set) for at least 30 days before you wallpaper them. Coat the new plaster with a primer and the plasterboard with a sealer before you start.

CAUTION: Turn off the electricity before you remove the switchplates, fixtures, and outlets.

5

TYPING RÉSUMÉS FOR A STEADY INCOME

If you are a good typist and can type correspondence, manuscripts, and reports, typing résumés professionally may be for you. An ad in the local newspapers will bring you the job-hunters. A job-hunter can be a recent graduate or a mature executive.

A good résumé, presented well, should give the prospective employer an overview of who they are interviewing at a glance, and you need to tailor it to that person's needs. There are many reasons a person needs a résumé, and here are a few hints on what constitutes a good résumé:

For the inexperienced job-hunter, use a sheet of 8½ × 11″ typing paper and place the name, address, and phone number at the top of each page.

The page should contain the following in outline form:

1. The job wanted (for example, sales representative)
2. Potential growth or goal (sales management)
3. Traits that demonstrate competency (ability to work well with others)
4. Personal information:
   a. Education: Schools, degrees, and number of years
   b. School memberships (extra curricular activities, if any)

    c. Any other information or talents (fluency in another language, willingness to relocate, free to travel)

For the experienced job-hunter, use a sheet of 8½ × 11" typing paper and place the person's name, address, and phone number at the top of the page.

The page should contain the following in outline form:

1. Present position (for example, plant manager)
2. Field of work (steel fabrication)
3. Responsibilities (erection of plants)
4. Personality traits (organizer)
5. Position desired (engineer)
6. Additional talents (fluency in languages)
7. Success stories (for example, how a plant was built)
8. Work history (most recent dates first)
9. Education (all schools and degrees with years, additional courses applying to career)
10. Willingness to relocate.

After the job hunter has given you the information required for the résumé, work it into the outline form.

Example of outline form:

```
NAME
ADDRESS
PHONE NUMBER

Manager
_____

Industrial Engineering
_____

Experience in:
_____
_____
_____

Knowledge of:
_____
_____
_____

Characteristics Pertinent to the Field
_____
_____
_____
```

Or, impress the prospective employer with this:

FOLD THE TYPEWRITER SHEET IN HALF

RESUME

NAME
ADDRESS
CITY/STATE
PHONE

FOLD

POSITION OBJECTIVE

AND NOW OPEN IT UP

RESUME _____ NAME

WORK EXPERIENCE   EDUCATION

_____ BUSINESS ORIENTED   _____ BUSINESS ORIENTED

_____ ART ORIENTED   _____ ART ORIENTED

                                   _____ OTHER

Many college graduates and executives cannot write a good business letter, so you may also be asked to write a *motivation letter*.

The Motivation Letter

A motivation letter is actually a résumé in letter form, addressed to the head of a company. It is sent without a résumé to try to get an interview.

At the interview, the résumé is available. If the traveling is too great for an interview, the résumé can be mailed on request.

A good motivation letter should begin with "Your organization may be in need of_____." The second paragraph states the person's present position and the position wanted. The succeeding paragraphs give programs and past successes. In the next to last paragraph give educational background and talents (such as public speaking, writing, fluency in languages). The last paragraph asks for an interview.

If you are asked to compose, not just type, the résumé and the motivation letter, take a deposit from your client, all the information, and have the job-hunter return in a couple of days. You will need time to evaluate the material, study your reference book, write, and then type.

An excellent how-to-book for résumés is *Résumés for the Job Hunter* by Maury Shykind, published by Arco Publishing Company, Inc. Your library or paperback store will have it.

6
IF I CAN GET 30 CENTS FOR EMPTY CANS HOW COME I'M WATCHING THE SOAPS?

Thirty cents for ten empty beer or soft drink cans! It's true! The price of aluminum has gone up so rapidly in the past several years, that it has reached the price of thirty cents a pound, which is what ten cans weigh.

Since recycling has become big business for the general public, I think you might want to take a closer look at this current bonanza.

Recycling has created a demand for used aluminum, old newspapers, cardboard boxes, and old magazines. Senior citizens' clubs and private groups can have their own collection programs. Now that the price has gone so high, you'll need either a car or two with a large trunk or a truck—if someone in your group has one—and a convenient collection place. If all your neighbors know that you or someone in the group will be collecting regularly, they will be eager to cooperate since each will share in the profits.

The Paper Recycling Committee of The American Paper Institute estimates that about 25 percent of the newspapers consumed in this country are recycled, a figure that currently falls short of the volume needed to meet projected demand.

Can you really make money fooling around with all this old stuff? In Sun City, Arizona, a group of six Lions Clubs banded together to operate a collection program for the community's 55,000 residents. They earned more than $8,000 a month for the support of local and national charity and to finance Lions Club activities.

The Paper Recycling Committee said a real need is for corrugated cardboard, with recycling payments as high as $40 and up per ton. It takes about 100 corrugated boxes to make up 100 pounds, or 2,000 boxes for a ton, and the current prices paid for old newspapers range up to $40 a ton.

Brochures with directions and suggestions on recycled paper collection for income are available free of charge for you from The American Paper Institute, Paper Recycling Committee, 260 Madison Avenue, New York, New York 10016.

7

GROWING CACTUS—
EASY TO GROW, EASY TO SELL

From Canada to Argentina, from sea level to the high mountains, in deserts or in dripping jungles, most all varieties of this large family of succulent plants will survive and thrive.

The smaller varieties that we are interested for profit can be grown indoors without the sun, outdoors in the sun or shade, in soil, sand, greenhouses, small spaces in small apartments, and in large areas of ground. A full-time dedicated grower with a good parcel of land can make up to $30,000 a year.

One of the most popular species bought by collectors and sold widely in most nurseries and supermarkets is *corypantha*. This little cactus is one of the hardiest and will take temperatures far below zero. The main body of the plant is usually from four to six inches tall, and cylindrical or globe-shaped. When it blooms, the flowers are like tiny wreaths arranged in a circle near the top of the plant, in glowing colors of red, pink, yellow, or white. As they grow, the bodies are covered with little knobs, sometimes as many as twenty to each plant. They grow in clusters around the bottom and are easily separated—this is where you cash in, and here is how you do it: Fill a nursery flat with sand, fertilize it with Miracle Gro, and make two-inch lines both horizontally and vertically so that you end up with two-inch squares. After you snap off the little knobs, place each one in a square and continue until the flat is full. Take care while handling the knobs as they are spiny, so use garden gloves or small strips of paper long enough to wrap around the knob and protect your hands.

If you are fortunate enough to have a small plot of ground to work with, simply leave all the rocks after removing the weeds and debris. Once the area is cleaned, soak thoroughly until the water penetrates the ground down to about three inches. When the soil becomes workable, rake it to make a slight slope to let the water run off for good drainage, make your rows, and plant.

Since most varieties of cactus can be sold commercially, call several nurseries in your area. Ask them which types are more saleable than others, and which kinds they would be interested in buying from you. Call or go into all the supermarkets and grocery stores, talk to the manager, and explain that you are a cactus grower, and if they will buy from you, you will package them in two- or four-inch plastic pots for resale. Don't be bashful, they buy from someone, so why not you?

If you sell to nurseries, most will supply you with the flats that they will sell them in. If you sell them otherwise, cactus will grow in just about any container, including milk cartons cut in half, with holes punched in them for drainage. A tall "bookcase effect" is desirable for keeping your plants free from harm until you are ready to market them. Do this by placing two bricks on the floor, put a board on top, two more bricks, another board, until the "bookcase" is as tall as you want it. This method can be used indoors or outdoors, and can be covered with a plastic drop cloth like painters use for a greenhouse effect.

Your original investment need not be more than a few dollars, and with lots of TLC (Tender Loving Care) you will find that some plants multiply quite rapidly, so that you can make that additional money fairly soon.

Growing cactus is fun and profitable, and remember that marketing your product is as simple as calling up the nursery, wholesaler, or supermarket and reporting that your plants are ready to sell. There are approximately 100 small plants in a nursery flat, and the selling price to you is around 50¢ each, so that each flat should bring you approximately $50. A small operation will easily net a thousand dollars a year, and if you can find some large plants (jade, for instance) that you can break up into small sections to start off with a bang, you will be able to make a lot more money.

II

Looking Ahead:
What to Do—
And How to Do It!

8

HOW TO SELL FOR PROFIT

Trying to decide what to do to make that extra money takes a lot of time and thought and some of this knowledge will come to you either from your own experiences or from hearing about what others have done. Use this knowledge to your advantage. Whether financial circumstances or boredom have forced you to make some extra money, here are some sound business procedures that you can use to start counting on, in addition to your own strength and initiative.

Here are some questions you might ask yourself:

1. Is there a hobby I'm doing right now that I can make a business of?
2. How much additional money do I need each month?
3. How much more preparation and training do I need?

Any product or service that you will be selling has to have a business license. Call your city licensing department for information on how to get one. They will not require you to go down there as you can do this by mail. To tell others who you are and what you are doing, print some cards with your name, address, and telephone number, plus the name of the business, and take them around to supermarkets, laundromats, the neighborhood, and to all the business places you feel might buy your product or service. Call, mail, or distribute all the advertising you can about your new venture. Talk to as many people as you can about yourself and what you are now doing. Talk to potential buyers and to people who will refer buyers to you. Some days you may only have a short time to contact people, but other days you will have several hours, as this is the hardest and most important groundwork that is so necessary for a very profitable future.

The nicest and sweetest boost of all is the free publicity through your local newspapers. Call your newspaper, introduce yourself, tell them what you are doing, and ask for an interview with one of their reporters. Local papers print new local interests, and since this is so important to you, keep trying and calling until you can get an appointment. This is a wonderful way to get the exposure that you need.

DECIDING ON THE SELLING PRICE

Since you need to make a profit, here is a very simple formula:

$$\text{selling price} - \text{total cost} = \text{profit}$$

If you aren't sure how to get the top price, try a few different ways at the beginning. One sure way is to sell more of a product with a smaller profit.

It's a lot more work to start a new business this way, but you will be busier and have a lot more enthusiasm, and your new business will grow by leaps and bounds as the word gets around; in no time the profits will be rolling in and you will laugh at how easy it all was as you look back at your struggling start.

Try to put the early profit back in the new venture. You will find that to have more volume you will have to have more things to sell. This is true whether you are baking cookies, doing art work, growing cactus, or producing anything that is to be sold at a wholesale or a retail level.

It won't take very long to know if you are on the right track, but don't get discouraged. If your price is too high, you will know all too soon in the lack of sales, so reduce your price and get you and your service or product known. As the demand grows, you can then raise your price accordingly. That is no different from a large firm that introduces a new product on the market at a reduced price to expose it to as many people as possible.

SELF-PROMOTION

A friendly, enthusiastic voice is contagious, so when you meet your prospective buyers, sell them on yourself before you show your product by voicing genuine appreciation for their giving you time from their busy day.

When we buy something for ourselves, we expect the store to stand in back of its merchandise and replace any wrong or damaged article immediately. Your customers will expect the same thing from you.

HOW TO GET AN ORDER

Trying to keep a positive attitude to give you the desire, drive, and confidence to succeed in your new venture is very difficult. Don't be discouraged if you don't sell your first prospects, because as you continue to contact people, selling *will* become easier and easier.

Never be afraid to ask people to buy. Most businesses start out in the very same way that you are, step by step. Talk about the exciting features of what you are doing, and always assure your customers that they will get their orders exactly as you represented them.

Asking questions that people will answer yes to is a positive way of closing your order without actually asking for the order. Use questions that end in "Isn't that so?" "Don't you agree?" "Wouldn't that be nice?" For example, you might say, "I could deliver these, if you needed them, in record time. Wouldn't that be nice?"

Have a well-thought out program of pricing. In order to quote prices on different quantities, work up a price sheet from a single unit to a dozen or more. Have these neatly hand printed or typed.

Don't be afraid to admit you don't know something about your product, and show concern about a person's need for the right timing on a delivery. All this shows your prospective buyers that you are a responsible person, concerned for their needs as well as your orders, and it will go a long step forward in getting you your first few orders.

9

CONSIDERING
A DIRECT-SALES JOB

When a person needs more income, he or she usually starts by looking in the want-ad section of the newspaper under employment opportunities. If nothing there seems to fill the bill, most of us will look over into the sales opportunities section, even though we have never sold anything in our lives. Most of the ads sound too good to be true. How can we resist ads that read "It's never too late to be your own boss," "Start your own career," "Be independent for life," "$500 to $1500 per week," and even "For a small investment ($350) you can join our team."?

When ads advertise for a "sales executive," "sales representative," or any other great-sounding position, they are attractive ways of saying that you would be selling for this company on a straight-commission basis only. This is no salary and no draw against future earnings. If you don't sell any of their products, you won't make any money! But—often there is no qualification for higher education and no sales experience required, so this could be just the spare-time job that you're looking for. You can pick your own time to work, decide on the number of hours you want to work, gain confidence, and make new friends.

Consider the risks in time and money. Some direct-sales companies say that the money you have to invest up front is minimal, that it is worth your time and effort to give it a try. The direct-sales market statistics tell us that there may be as many as three million women working for direct-sales companies. These women are selling cookware, jewelry, cosmetics, clothing, and more. A large amount of your clientele will be working women who can see your products only at night. Plan on spending every weekend working, because that is the best time to see most busy working women. They appreciate the convenience of personal attention and enjoy the leisure pace this affords them.

DIRECT SALES

Door-to-Door Selling

Direct-sales companies generally use two basic selling plans: the door-to-door plan and the party plan. Probably the more lucrative is door-to-door selling. Products sold this way are those that people need all the time: soap, colognes, vitamins, vacuum cleaners, brushes, and cosmetics. You call on your customers again and again, so you have a continuous repeat-order business. You need a strong constitution for this type of selling, and it takes a lot of getting used to. A door slammed in the face more than once intimidates most people, especially the timid types. Most companies, however, often try to provide a few good leads and maybe an established customer or two to get the newcomer started.

In the beginning, you will start by asking your family and friends for orders, and then—the reality sets in and the real hard work begins. Some direct-sales women say that door-to-door selling gets easier after about two years. By that time you will probably be working fewer hours and making much more money. If you don't have access to a car, you can work in your neighborhood. With an admirable frankness, neither Avon nor Fuller Brush claims to be a big-money opportunity. They project earnings for their reps to be between $6 and $8 per hour.

Avon pays a commission of about 40 percent, and Fuller Brush pays about 35 percent on orders for more than $125. You can, of course, work all of the time you have to spare. The more customers that you have means the more money that you will make.

Usually, door-to-door companies encourage "recruiting"—convincing new people to work for your company. You will earn a percentage of the new person's commissions.

There are many ways to increase your clientele. Leave your brochures in supermarkets, post notices in laundromats, devote an hour each day to calling potential customers (weekday evenings and Saturdays are best), pass out flyers in your neighborhood introducing yourself. Because your business depends on repeat sales, you will call back on the same customers.

When you sell door to door, you have a high potential for large profits and the advantage of choosing your own hours. However, this type of selling calls for high levels of self-discipline and self-motivation. The largest group of drop-outs is made up of women who are sole supporters of families.

The Party Plan

The party plan is a lot more popular with most women because you can combine work with pleasure. The parties are not given by you in your home, but by a hostess whom you have recruited to do this for you. The hostess invites her friends and relatives and gets a gift from you for her help. She also can increase the value of her gift by the amount of money generated from the orders you write up during the party. More hostesses can be recruited from the audience to give their own parties.

That's all there is to the party plan. The concept is somewhat like a chain letter—from the first party the hostess gives comes the opportunity to gather a few more hostesses. The hostesses are happy with their gifts. The parties go on and on, and you will be happily writing up sales orders. The hostesses can, of course, also become salespeople, and if they sell anything you will get a percentage of their commissions.

The effort that is put out in this endeavor is constant. Your time is not your own and all of your evenings are taken. The telephone will ring constantly, and you will need a large car to transport your products and gifts. You can, of course, work only part time, but this may quickly become a full, ongoing job with a large commitment.

Before you get involved with any company or plan, talk to a few people who are already doing this type of work. If you answer any of the ads, find out what the company is doing and try checking up on the program yourself before you make any commitment. Find out how much you can make if you work part time. If you are recruited to work for a company, the recruiter's profits will depend on the commissions that you make, so find out what you want to know. If you feel comfortable with the recruiter, ask if you can attend a few parties with her.

Take your time in joining the company—it could turn out to be an expensive commitment.

The company you choose to work for will probably furnish you with all the sales tools you need. This package may include a sales manual, sales kits containing product samples, and brochures to pass out to your trade. The more elaborate the sample kit is, the more it will cost you to buy; however, the kits are usually sold to you at a discount from the regular price, and you won't have to put out all the money at once.

One of the largest direct-sales companies has a kit valued at $400. Your cost for this sample kit is about $175. You pay $25 initially and the balance comes out of your first commission check. Some direct-sales companies have kits worth $400 and they give you this sample merchandise for $100, payable when you make your first sale. None of the monies you pay up front are refundable, and you may still owe the balance of the sample kit if you decide that you don't like the job. Based on the amount of time it takes you to get your commission check from the time you send in your orders, you must plan on extra out-of-pocket money that could go as high as $200. These are extra expenses you have at first until your checks start coming in—shipping charges, order forms, telephone calls, packaging supplies, gasoline for your car, and lunches out.

The reason that the drop-out rate is so high among beginners is the fact that this work is *hard*. The staggeringly high income that the ads tell you that you *can* make should tell you that you will have to put in a lot of hours—many more than the 30 hours you may have originally planned on. Although the ad says that some people make a six-figure income, you will find that the really big money comes from recruiting women who will work for you as hostesses and saleswomen. This is the only way to make those big bucks—get a percentage of what "your group" earns from their commissions!

Check out the company—how good are the guarantees? How do they handle returns? It is important to know how they handle your orders and how much time it takes from the time you submit the order to the time you receive it. No customer will wait forever for her order, and you can lose before you start.

In the following list are firms that you can call (many are toll-free) for any information that you might need. For a directory of more than 100 firms, write to the Direct Selling Association, 1730 M Street, NW, Washington, D.C., 20036.

DIRECT SALES FIRMS

All American Toy (801-375-7200): stuffed animals and novelties; party plan.

Amway (616-676-6000): household products; person-to-person.

Avon (800-227-3737; in California call 800-652-1554): cosmetics and other products; person-to-person.

Beeline Fashions (312-860-3200): clothing; party plan.

Creative Expression (215-693-3191): craft products; party plan.

Doncaster (704-287-4205): clothing; person-to-person.

Electrolux (800-243-9078; in Connecticut call 800-942-0327): vacuums and related items; person-to-person.

Encyclopaedia Britannica (312-321-7000): reference books; person-to-person.

Fuller Brush (816-474-1754): household products; person-to-person.

Hanover Shoes (717-632-7575): work and dress shoes; person-to-person.

Home Interiors & Gifts (214-386-1000): decorative accessories; party plan.

Mary Kay (800-527-6270; in Texas call 800-442-5473): skin-care products; party plan.

Princess House (800-343-5490): crystal and decorative accessories; party plan.

Sarah Coventry (800-448-9638; in New York call 800-962-9656): jewelry; party plan.

Stanley Home Products (800-628-9032; in Massachusetts call 800-332-3831): household items; party plan.

Tupperware (305-847-3111): household products; party plan.

Vollrath (414-457-4851): cookware, both plans.

Watkins (507-457-3300): specialty food items; both plans.

10

STARTING YOUR OWN MAIL ORDER BUSINESS!

This chapter tells you how to start a business in your own home. Watch the checks from your customers flow in!

Mail order revenues in the United States amount to about $60 million a year—generated by about 7,500 mail outlets. Why is it so lucrative?

First, it is so convenient for the shopper. This is armchair shopping—no hassle of crowded stores and wasted time.

Second, there is the selection of hard-to-get unique items, especially in rural and suburban areas far removed from specialty shops.

Third, mail order shopping is economical—no carfare, no gasoline, and no store overhead. Frequently, mail ordering is cheaper than purchasing the same items in the store—if you can find them! Before we go on to specific business methods, let us define three often-confused terms. Mail order really has three different components—direct mail, mail order, and direct marketing.

1. *Direct mail* is an advertising method. The advertiser sends letters or catalogues directly to potential customers.
2. *Mail order* is a marketing method by which the potential customer receives the *news* of the product—either by direct mail

or in an advertisement, sends back an order form and check by mail, and then receives the product by any suitable means of transportation.

3. *Direct marketing* is a broad marketing method that includes all promotion—such as TV advertising and coupons mailed to the customer.

STARTING OUT

If you are a typical beginner, you operate from your own home, possibly on a part-time basis at first. You are learning at the least expense, promoting only one or two articles by advertising in a publication or by direct mail. Once you know the ins and outs and start to show a little profit, you can enlarge with more products and a larger customer list. There are two other good ways of starting—if you have the money. Buy out another mail order firm or join an already established retail store and run the mail order end to get the experience to start your own mail order business.

However, let us start with you, a beginner operating in your own home. Before you do anything, research the legal requirements in your state:

1. Contact your local Federal Trade Commission (FTC) office and ask for a list of their publications or any publication dealing with the mail order business.

2. Write to the General Post Office in Washington, D.C. and ask for the postal service manual that contains all of the postal regulations.

3. If you plan to have an employee to help you, contact the Internal Revenue Service. You will be assigned an employer's identification number for income tax withholding and social security taxes.

4. Your State Department of Benefit Payments will give you a number for the state withholding taxes and disability insurance (again, if you hire an employee).

5. Your state Board of Equalization will issue you a seller's permit after you register at your local office.

Because you are a beginner in the marketing field, you must also check:

Fictitious Name Registration: Your state will require you to register your new name of the company, and require you to publish this in the county newspaper.

Local Zoning Regulations: Depending upon the product, there is a possibility that the zoning laws may or may not permit you to operate your mail order business in your own home.

Property taxes: If you run a business in your home, you may be taxed according to the current tax table.

Business licenses: Some cities and counties require you to get a business license. This can be done in one visit to your city hall.

Once you have all the legal information, you can go on to your investment requirements, or *capital*.

One of the big plusses of the mail order business is that you need no substantial investment for rent, salaries, or products. By starting in your home, you need no money for rent, furniture, utilities, not even a business phone. You even deduct from income tax the maintenance and depreciating business expenses. While you are starting, you can hold another job until you are established. You can make or buy small amounts of your products until the orders increase.

You ask then—how much capital do I need to start up a mail order business? Your biggest expense is for the advertising. Other expenses include shipping, licenses, postage, insurance, taxes, and a little extra money in reserve for a possible beginner's mistake.

A survey of the mail order business indicates that with $5,000 you can start off as a beginner; $10,000 is a very adequate cushion. However, if you are going into the apparel business, you will need a capital outlay of from $25,000 to $50,000.

Still determined to start your mail order business in your own home? If you need *financing*, here are some choices:

Most mail order beginners usually depend on their own personal savings or a loan from family or friends. Banks will loan about 50 percent of the amount required if you can convince the lender that as a merchandiser you show some expertise. The Small Business Administration does make direct loans, but usually guarantees your loan made by the bank.

If you are going to apply to your bank for a loan, be prepared to furnish the following:

1. A résumé detailing your background, education, and business experience.
2. A statement of your personal financial status. Prepare a detailed plan for your mail order venture, projecting your expenses and income for the first and second years.
3. If you are going to take over an operating company, you need the financial records of the previous three years.

CHOOSING YOUR PRODUCT

Choosing a product or a project to make (or buy) is the most important step in your new mail order operation. *Everything* that you do depends on the successful marketability of your item or items!

In the search for new and unique ideas, you can do the following:

1. Attend trade shows in major cities if you can. Check with the trade associations, and watch for shows advertised in your local paper.
2. In the big cities, look in the yellow pages for manufacturers and lists of suppliers. The public library has, or can obtain for you, manufacturers' directories, McRaes Blue Book, or the Thomas Register of American Manufacturers. You can also find the American Register of Exporters and Importers.

In selecting your saleable item, you can either introduce an established item to a new market, personalize an ordinary item, or handicraft your own special original idea and market it by mail.

BUYING A PRODUCT FOR RESALE

When you buy another's product for resale through a mail order business, have a firm price commitment from the manufacturer for a payment schedule and delivery dates. To begin with, you will probably be required to pay cash, and later be able to make arrangements for a discount if paid in ten days. You need a small inventory to start with and a firm commitment from your supplier that he or she can quickly ship you additional stock if you need it. A small manufacturer may agree to ship an order on consignment. With this method of buying you do not have to pay for the item until it is sold.

ADVERTISING YOUR PRODUCT

The money spent on advertising is the biggest expense. But remember you have *no* other means of reaching your buyers!

You can decide on a *direct mail letter* or an ad in the local newspapers. You can use daily, weekly, or monthly publications. Select your advertising according to the type of product you are selling and the people you want to reach. You might even consider women's magazines, home and apartment magazines, business and news publications, special interest magazines (such as sports, psychology) and mass circulation weeklies (such as *The Enquirer*).

All of these publications are terribly expensive, and not for the rank beginner, so to test your advertising in publications, start out with small ads. You may even find a 50 percent discount for what is known as a *remnant space*. This is space left over on a page, not completely filled by advertisers paying the regular price.

You may decide on *direct mail advertising*, but this consists of a letter or brochure, order forms, reply cards, and return envelopes, and it may be too large a project to start out with if you have no previous experience. Also, unless you really know the advertising business, you have to work with an advertising agency to create an attractive direct mail order ad.

Timing is all important. Christmas items, for instance, are advertised no later than September, spring and summer items are advertised by January. Three months is the usual time period used to allow the browser to place the order with you and for you to ship back the merchandise. Whatever method you use, keying or coding must be used in your order forms. For your records you should know from what ad and when your order came—for instance, LHJ3 would mean the *Ladies' Home Journal*, March edition.

KEEPING BUSINESS RECORDS

All stationery stores have small, compact journals for you to use to keep track of your new business venture. This bookkeeping system includes all of your inventory purchases (the shipments you receive), accounts payable (money you owe), and accounts receivable (money due you).

Keep a daily tabulation (record) made from customer remittances, purchase orders, check stubs, petty cash receipts, invoices, and, if you employ anyone, payroll vouchers. A daily record is just like a running inventory; you always know what is going on and will be able to control your outgoing money.

Daily, in a permanent ledger, enter the income and expense figures. *You will need these records at income tax time!* You will also need these figures of incoming and outgoing monies as a guide for future planning.

In the mail order business, it is necessary to keep current two special files:

1. *The Customer File*: Using plain index cards, enter your customer's name, address, order date, amount of purchase, shipping dates, and the keyed advertisement (telling you from which ad the customer got your address to order your product).

2. *An Advertising Tally Sheet*: This is the daily record that counts the orders from your advertising key (telling you if it was worth the money to run that particular ad). A separate record is also needed to count the number of orders received from a specific ad in one year.

Forecasts for the mail order business: The consensus of industry observers is that the mail order business will remain, for both large and small mailers, bright and expanding! For the larger mailers, computers will cut costs. For the smaller mailer, rising postal costs may require careful budget management.

The much-touted shopping-at-home by computer, video, cablevision, or picture phones are a long way off. There are still at least ten years ahead for the shrewd merchandiser to reach the customer in the mail order business. So get started, and you can expect to prosper in the years ahead!

11

DECORATING FOR DOLLARS

Decorating, like writing or painting, is an art. Many people have a natural talent for decorating, and can create a pleasing look to their own home or apartment or to someone else's living quarters for a nice steady income. There is a marketplace for those talents in today's business world, so practice on your friends and neighbors first to gain skill and confidence.

Professional decorators can charge $35 or more per hour, or perhaps add a percentage on the total price of the custom furniture, rugs, etcetera, that their clients buy. Trips to the nearest furniture mart is where they buy their merchandise, and contacts with a good carpet and drapery installer is a must. Easy steps are outlined here for you to follow:

SIMPLIFIED USE OF COLOR

Colors transform dull and dingy rooms into an attractive background for living. The choice of a color is always personal, but here are a few basic rules that should help govern that choice:

Start out with a few colors rather than too many.
Use lighter colors rather than darker ones.

Rooms with northern exposures need warmer colors, and rooms with southern exposures need cooler colors.

For larger areas, use lighter colors with strong accents of color.

The lightest color in your color scheme should go on the wall, and next-lightest and intermediate tones can be used for the draperies.

Colors create different moods. For example, blues, greens, cream, and shades of brown and white create a mood of serenity. Others are dramatic and should be used sparingly in a large room. These colors include red, orange, royal blue, hot pink, and any color that does not produce an atmosphere of harmony. For example, in a home with brown carpets and a southern exposure, use cool colors on the wall. Accent colors of pale blue, moss green, turquoise, and white are very effective. For rooms that are dark, use light beige on the walls, with accents of cocoa brown, cream, tan, coral, or yellow. In a room with only artificial lighting, cozy it up with tan walls, accents of rust, terra cotta, and pale green for a rich, warm feeling. The use of color is of vital importance in decorating a home. Color can pull together all the elements of a room and make defects less apparent. In a small home colors well used can create a sense of spaciousness.

Draperies

There is nothing that will give a room a more finished look than draperies or curtains. Without them a room is cold and uninviting, but with them the room becomes warm and appealing. Depending on the sizes of the windows and the room and the kind of a mood you want to create, you can use drapery fabrics of antique, casements (loosely woven weaves), sheers, sheets, plus synthetic fabrics.

Drapery Lengths

There are only three basic drapery lengths to worry about when you measure the room for draperies; floor length, which is usually 84" long; sill length, which is ¼" to ½" above the sill and ½" above the drapery rod; and apron length, which is 2" below the apron and ½" above the rod.

To give the illusion of height to a room, hang the drapes from the floor to the ceiling. It is extremely important to have your drapes made at least two times the width of your window in each panel. When the drapes are drawn you will have a full, custom look; otherwise you will have a skimpy drape that looks stretched to its limit when closed. Full draperies cut down on outside noise and keep the home cooler in the summer and warmer in the winter. The finished length of your floor-to-ceiling drape is ½" from the carpet. If there is no carpet down as yet, ask for a sample of the carpet and measure it. The general rule is 1" less at the bottom for new carpeting and 2" for shag rugs.

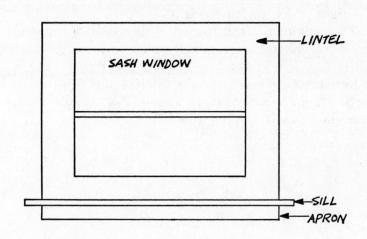

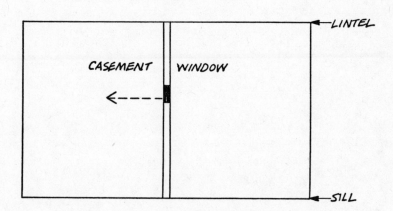

Drapery Rods

Fashions in rods may be determined by the style and design in architecture, so when it comes to the different window treatments, there is no hard-and-fast rule. The size and shape of the windows, the absence of a view, and the colors of the rug and furniture will all have a bearing on what you decorate a window with. Drapery rods are usually installed 4" above the top of the window and 4" out from each side of the window. The most popular and best rod for draperies is the traverse rod. This rod is adjustable for both the ceiling and wall attachments. The box comes complete with the cord pulleys and the plastic slides. The traverse rod comes in many sizes to fit any window and solves the problem of whether the drape opens from the middle (center pull) or is a one-way draw (right to left or left to right).

If you paint the rod to match the color of the walls, it will blend in nicely and won't stand out. Always hang the drapes so that the top hem is at least ½" above the rod to hide it.

Here are two books that the interested reader can look to for help: *Starting From Scratch* by Joanna Barnes, and *Easy Steps to Successful Decorating* by Barbara Bradford.

12

IF YOU CAN PAINT, EXTRA DOLLARS ARE YOURS!

Would you, an artist, like to earn your extra income by painting? Here is how!

Two things are necessary to sell a painting. You must show it where a number of people can see it, and you must price it so that almost anyone who wants to buy it, can.

HOW TO SHOW YOUR PAINTINGS

1. *Small City*: Start with your local bookstore. Browsing, customers will look at your paintings. Bookstores can use the extra income by acting as your agent (for a fee, usually one-third of the price).

   A tourist gift shop is another outlet. If you live in a tourist area, paint the local attraction—be it a mountain or historical building. Paint it over and over in different sizes using oils or watercolors. Finish up by putting some paintings in mats or frames as needed. You are then in the $6.50 to $50 class, and, although you may not feel like a Rembrandt, you will sell some of your paintings.

2. *Rural Area*: Here you can set up a roadside exhibit with signs well in advance. Display some paintings at your front door for passers-by to see.

    Statistically, one in fifty passers-by stop to look, and about one of eight lookers will buy. That means that you will make one sale for every 400 people who pass by. Try to exhibit on a busy street.

3. *Large City*: Your agent can be your bookstore, gift shop, local department store, or furniture shop. A picture-framing shop could be a place for you to swap services either for framing or selling art.

Watercolors already matted can be displayed in a rack ready for framing. Ready-framed oils should have their hanging wire placed so the purchaser can take it home and hang it.

Visit an interior decorator's shop. He or she will know of people who are redecorating who want paintings, and businesspeople who need prints for their offices.

Note: Remember that if your paintings are placed with a selling agent on consignment, your payment is usually two-thirds of the selling price. If two or more people sell your painting, they split the one-third fee.

Get the agreement with your agent in writing, and get a receipt of the size, title, description, and price of all paintings. Keep a record of each painting completed giving the title, to whom consigned, date consigned, date sold, price received, and who bought it.

HOW TO PRICE YOUR PAINTINGS

Take three of your paintings and rank and price each—say, $25, $50, and $100. See how they sell. Oils usually sell faster and at higher prices than watercolors and drawings do. Your more-quickly completed watercolor may sell for $15, but it may sell faster than the oil that took a month to complete. Your goal is to make money, so don't worry about being a "hack." Turn out the paintings to sell—you can at the same time be working on that oil to sell for over $100.

SHOULD YOU MAT OR FRAME?

In the lower price ranges, matted paintings sell better—the buyer wants a lower price and plans eventually to do the framing himself. For a higher-priced painting, especially an oil, the right frame can make a difference. But do not tie up money in framing. Try one oil and see what happens.

Note: If your paintings are piling up at your agent's, reduce the prices. If you have only a few left, raise the prices. Use standard-size canvases so your agent can assure buyers that standard (much cheaper) frames are readily available. In the corner of the painting, on a 2 × 4″ card, give the title and price. Decide with your agent if a painting may be purchased on an installment plan.

COMMISSIONED PAINTINGS

Someone who sees your painting of a house, garden, or animal may ask you to do his house, garden, or animal. You arrive at a price, take a deposit—but beware! Your client may not see his possessions as you, the artist, see them. He or she may criticize, ask for adjustments. If you cannot agree, keep your good humor, give back the deposit, and sell the painting to someone else.

Paint what you like to paint—romanticize, satirize; use violent colors, paint soft sunsets—there is always someone who will like what you believe in. But never forget you are painting—not for fame—but for those extra dollars you want!

13

CUSTOMIZED POSTAL SERVICE

The charge today for a U.S. Post Office mailbox is $1.69 per month. Sometimes there are no available boxes for rent and people have no choice but to wait for the next available box.

This is where you come in: A private custom postal service business is an ideal alternative for this problem as you can offer a 24-hour service for people to pick up their mail and packages.

The rate for this is:

> Small postal box: $10.00 per month
>
> Medium postal box: $15.00 per month
>
> Large postal box: $20.00 per month
>
> *Note*: All box rentals are for a three-month minimum.

The larger amount for a private postal service is accepted by persons who have a job that would require them to travel a lot, who prefer a postal box number with a street address, or those who wish to change their postal box number into a suite number. Renting a mailbox is a personal affair and there are many different reasons for doing so.

Depending on where you live and the lifestyle of the people around you, people who need the conveniences of a savings both in time and money will gladly pay a higher price than the U.S. Postal service charges.

To be successful in a business like this one, you should be in an area with a good location and some parking space, even if the cars can only park there a few minutes. A small rental business in a shopping center would be ideal, however, you can use part of your home or garage for this type of business, but be sure to check this out with your zoning laws.

Whether you live in the city or the country, consider having the mailboxes in a spare room with an outside entrance or a garage. It may not be necessary to provide mail service for boxes with a lid and key. You might want to have a wall covered with open numbered compartments.

You can buy or build about 300 postal boxes in a very small space. A standard post office box is approximately 4″ by 8″ and 12″ deep; however, you can make the boxes any size you wish. A 6′ by 6′ wall space will accommodate approximately 125 mailboxes. You can charge $15 to $20 a month for larger boxes for customers who have lots of mail.

The gross income for 300 box rentals is at least $3000 a month. You will have the initial expenses of having the mailboxes built, the keys made, and so on. (See your Small Business Administration for a loan if you have contacted two other lending institutions and they have turned you down).

Enterprising postal service businesses also provide service for their customers that bring in extra money. These extra moneymaking supplements include:

1. Private mailboxes with a street address: People can pick up their mail and packages at any time of the day or night. (Your office hours are from 9 to 5, but the people who rent the mailboxes have a key to get in the part of the building where the mailboxes and packages are kept).

2. Telephone answering service: Your customers can leave messages 24 hours a day. Charge per month: $5.00.

3. Stamps and letters: Save them a trip to the Post Office. Sell stamps as a convenience and drop off their letters at the Post Office for them. (No profit here, but lots of good will).

4. Package delivery: You pick the best carrier so the package arrives when your customers want it to. use U.P.S., Federal

Express, United Air Express, Airborne, or others in your area. Accept packages also for your customers so that they won't waste time waiting for deliveries. Handling charge per package should be $1.50 and up, depending on the size.

5. Packaging and packaging supplies: The contents of the packages are left with you, and you do the rest. Use professional materials so the package arrives at its destination in good condition. Charge for packaging materials: $2.50 each box. Charge for handling: $1.50 each box.

6. Copies: Use a high-quality bond paper. This service is available to anyone who wishes the service during the hours of 9 to 5, and only to your customers after hours. Charge per copy: $.10 per copy. Less on volume.

7. Secretarial services: Find someone who can type professionally and offer fast, accurate typing for letters, résumés, transcripts, and even answering your customers' mail. Charge for page, depending on the contents: $1.50 to $2.50.

8. Business cards and stationery: Contact your local printer and set up an agreement for them for a percentage of the cost of the order.

9. Keys made: $1.00 per key.

10. Rubber stamps: See your local printer for this.

11. Contact your nearest Western Union and see if you can make arrangements for candy and flowergrams, cablegrams, money orders, and telegrams.

12. You can also enlarge this small but lucrative business with part of the store space given over to boutique items, notary services, or office supplies. Think about all of the extra services you would like if someone around you opened this type of small business and then add it to your list of possibilities for the future. It's never too late!

14

COSMETOLOGY FOR DOLLARS IN YOUR OWN HOME

If you have experience in any of the related fields of beauty care, your home can be your own dollar-making salon for other senior women.

You can arrange appointments in your home, at your own pace—no long hours on your feet. Clients can be neighbors, making a shampoo or manicure a social event over a cup of coffee. Your discount price for beauty services to other senior women can be attractive.

Before you start, check your location:

1. In a rural area, parking facility is important.
2. In a city area, you may need access to public transportation.
3. Proximity to shops and services is an advantage.
4. Apartment or condo complexes have a sufficient population of homemakers and retired women for daytime appointments.

CHECKING YOUR HOME

As in a salon, you will need:

1. A reception area with a congenial atmosphere (your living room).
2. A styling station: A chair before an adequate mirror with good lighting (dressing table and supply cabinet in your bedroom or living room).
3. A shampoo area: Bowl with spray and chair to accommodate the shampoo tray (your bathroom).
4. A storage area: Shelves and drawers to accommodate your supplies (a section of your kitchen cabinet and drawers).

BUILDING UP A CLIENTELE

In a beauty business, most new appointments are generated by referrals from satisfied customers. To start, talk to friends and neighbors and have inexpensive cards printed to give out at church and social events, senior citizen affairs, and to put in mailboxes. A small ad in your local newspaper is an excellent start. Your important message will be your discount price as compared to salon prices. Your prices should be posted in the reception area and included on your business cards and ads.

EQUIPMENT

Your home equipment will be minimal if you plan to only shampoo, set, blow dry, and manicure.

Hard goods include hand dryer, bouffant hair dryer, manicure table and supplies, chairs, and shampoo tray.

Soft goods include shampoos, rinses, lotions, sprays, and conditioners. Soft goods purchased in large, economical containers can be transferred to convenient small containers.

Sundries: Sundries can be ordered through a local general supply house (yellow pages). These salon marts, stocking everything from shampoos to dryers, are more convenient than manufacturers. Deliveries are usually prompt and a 1 percent or 2 percent discount is usually offered for payment within ten days of billing.

FINANCING

A home-based service business such as your home hair grooming parlor may have trouble getting financial assistance. However, your local bank may give you a personal loan (if you have a savings or checking account). See your supply house, get a written estimate of the equipment and supplies you require, and present your bank with a businesslike proposition. You may find financing at a very low interest rate using your own account as collateral. Until you are launched successfully, experts advise no more than 50 percent of your equipment be financed by a loan.

SATISFIED CUSTOMERS

More customers are dissatisfied by poor personal treatment than by a mishap such as a too-short haircut or frizzy curls. A calm, friendly attitude and an effort to please will keep a client from walking out in anger. If a client selects a picture of a fashionable hair style, try to duplicate it as closely as possible but point out first that you cannot work a miracle on her particular type of hair. Appointments should be run on time to avoid an irritating wait. If you should meet with real dissatisfaction, offer one free corrective appointment or offer to refund the money. The client will spread the news of your reliability and friendliness.

RETAILING BEAUTY AIDS

A subtle soft-sell approach is a display case of products placed so the client can see it while she is under the dryer. Products related to your services, so temptingly visible, can be shampoos, conditioners, blow-dryers. Include rinses, moisturizers, cosmetics, combs and brushes. Salons are even displaying and selling vitamins, costume jewelry, and scarves.

In rural areas, about 12 percent of cosmetology is done by solo women—usually in the home. Clients appreciate the accessibility of grooming products and gifts.

NEW DEVELOPMENTS

The fashionable look today is natural, manageable hair with the sheen of health. Gone is the bouffant look, the set look, the "tortured" look (overdyed, overfrizzed, etc.). Fashion is what looks best on the client.

PAMPERING YOUR CLIENT

Your client will be a visitor in your home. A smiling greeting, calling the customer by name, hanging a coat on the rack, and providing interesting magazines near the hair dryer are ways of saying "Come again!"

You can provide a dressing gown for your client (flower-fresh from your laundry room).

Keep on hand inexpensive plastic rain scarves to protect your styling from sudden rain or wind. Coffee, ash trays and dimes (in the city) for the meter are thoughtful touches. Always have on hand a few current hair fashion magazines to help you confer on styling.

A real hazard of a service in your home is gossip! Listen—but never, never pass on what you have heard to another client.

TRENDS

Ten years ago, the cut-and-blow dry technique began to change the ways of beauty salons. Haircutting for the blow-dry fashion required more expertise. Women now wash and blow-dry their own hair, sometimes daily. They go to the salon only every six or eight weeks instead of keeping a standing weekly appointment.

With soft body permanents and conditioners and color rinses, women no longer need have a stiff, drab look, adding years to an older face.

The cosmetologist today not only styles but treats hair—and statistics show that growing numbers of women, including senior women, want not only a hairdresser, but a mini-paraclinic for hair care. The new emphasis on healthy hair will continue. As one expert predicts, in spite of inflation or recession, "Women will eat less cake to pay for their hairdresser!" The combination of providing beauty styles and health products will continue into billions of dollars of annual sales.

You can be part of it in your own home!

The following sources of information will be helpful:

(Your state) State Board of Cosmetology

(Telephone information service to your state capital)

American Hairdresser/Salon Owner
100 Park Avenue, Suite 850
New York, N.Y. 10017

Modern Beauty Shop Magazine
300 West Adams Street
Chicago, Ill. 60606

15

MODERNIZING
THE FLOWER BUSINESS

Women today are doing a thriving business with a new innovative style of caring for and delivering flowers. These women are not sitting around waiting for customers to drop into their florist shops or waiting for the telephone to ring; they are going out after the business with services that have given their customers the custom touch they love.

You can be just like the milkman and deliver bunches of flowers between the hours of 7 and 9 in the morning at your customer's doorstep.

If you live in a city that has its own flower marketplace, you can go there at least three times a week and carry away the freshest picks of the season; otherwise contact a florist wholesaler to make your different selections.

Average charges: One bunch a week: $45 a month
                    Two bunches a week: $80 a month

INTERIOR PLANTSCAPING

The same amount of success can be gained by placing and caring for plants in professional or business offices. Look in the phone book to find the names you need and mail out cards advertising what it is that you do.

Your inventory will include from one to fifteen gallon plants in either hanging baskets or floor plants. Your customers will delight in always having fresh plants around to look at, never having to water them and getting the plants replaced if they get droopy.

After you deliver the plants, properly hang them from the ceilings or place them around the floors in a lovely basket container. Take weekly care of these plants by watering, feeding, and general doctoring.

The main business will be in leasing the plants, although you might place a small, discreet price tag on the plant should someone wish to purchase it from you.

Start small and the *only* thing that will make you any different from anyone else in the flower delivery business is *service*.

A lot of money can be made by decorating a church or a reception hall for weddings, parties, and holidays. You'll eventually need a large selection of popular and rare varieties. Maybe nobody promised you a rose garden, but if you have a green thumb, you can make your own!

16

PLANTS FOR RENT

A coleus never grows leggy, nor does a fern become droopy, for a real "green-thumber!"

All plants thrive with care. The philodendron keeps producing new bright-green leaves, the ficus benjaminas are not temperamental, and the grape ivies stay healthy.

The green boom is here to stay. Green-thumbers cater to the demand for a plant or two to liven up professional offices, stores, and doctors' waiting rooms.

As new as these women might be to the business world, they are fortified with the experience of their lifelong successes with greenery. They are now readily responding to the challenge of mixing business with pleasure!

A word of caution: This may not be a business venture that you can do alone. A friend or two may be needed. A station wagon or large car is needed to haul all the equipment it takes to care for the rented plants. The plants are in different environments. You need to be aware of such factors as air conditioning, artificial lighting, hot east or west exposures, plus the fact that potting soils are natural dumping grounds for leftover coffee and other refuse.

The attractive part of a plant rental business is the small overhead it takes to get started. You can start with a small route. For several months try five or ten customers at the most, and then increase the number if you can.

Your reputation and success will depend on the quality of the plants you purchase to use as rentals. Indoor plants come in a large variety. The standard ornamental plants are, however, the ones that your customers will identify with.

A BEGINNER'S BASIC INVENTORY

Hanging Plants

Hanging plants include philodendrons, grape ivies, English ivies, and baltica—which is similar to English ivy except that the leaves turn purple in winter. Also consider variegated Algerian ivy—a miniature leaved form that adapts well for a filler in smaller pots, creeping charlies, ferns of all types, piggybacks, and spider plants.

Potted Floor Plants

Dracaena godsefiana is slow-growing and smaller than other dracaenas. It has slender, erect, and spreading stems set with pairs of dark-green leaves spotted with white.

Dieffenbachia (dumb cane) is an indoor plant with striking variegated leaves. The colors range from chartreuse to yellow, yellow-green, or dark green.

Ficus benjamina (weeping Chinese bamboo) is the number-one choice among interior decorators and landscapers. It is fast becoming the most popular ornamental plant to be used in any decor. Its graceful beauty is highly effective as an indoor plant.

Ficus elastica (rubber plant) is a familiar, foolproof houseplant that is found in offices all over the country. The leaves are thick and glossy. It is used mostly as a small tree or shrub, five to six feet in height. It looks great in a bamboo floor pot and can be used to landscape a shaded entrance to outdoors. It should be cut back periodically, though—if left alone, this plant could reach forty feet!

Schefflera (Queensland umbrella tree) is a sturdy evergreen indoor plant. It has tiers of long-stalked leaves that are divided into eight to ten leaflets that look like the ribs of an umbrella. Schefflera is also used sometimes with other plants, such as ferns, for a foliage contrast.

When you are purchasing the plants, look over the supply carefully. Buy only what you think a particular client will like. Don't overbuy and don't be pressured into buying something that

you are not sure you want. You may end up with too many dupli-
cates that way. As your plants grow too large, you will replace
them with the same type of plant or something similar. These
larger plants do nicely in larger offices.

Before you set up any shop, research the nearby suppliers
and find one that will sell you plants at a reasonable price. A plant
rental business is expected to supply top-notch plants to their
customers. Your selection cannot include damaged or unhealthy
plants. Just remember to be flexible in your selection of plants in
the beginning.

Look in the Yellow Pages of the telephone book for lists of
suppliers of gardening items. As the business grows, you will be
able to buy the materials you need in bulk, which will save you a
lot of money.

Some of the items you will need to keep your inventory green
and healthy are fertilizers, plant foods, potting soil, decorative
rock, hanging planters, floor pots, plus a good gardening book. You
also need to find companies that sell macramé hangers, plastic
and wood pots, and terrarium containers.

All businesses are sporadic at first. You can help it along by
contacting a few professional offices at first, telling them that you
have plants to rent. For many busy professional people, renting
plants for their waiting rooms is preferable to buying their own.
They don't have to worry about someone taking care of the greenery. Over 80 percent of the plants in professional offices are rented.

Normally, a hanging plant rents for $10 a month. Floor plants
range from $15 for a medium-sized plant to $20 for a stately plant
that will reach up to 8' in height.

Remember all of your expenses when you figure up the
charge for your plants: the initial cost of the plant, the price of the
container, the good soil and food, delivery and pick-up of the
plants, labor, and time.

Should your customers wish to purchase a plant instead of
renting it, you can sell it. You should charge three times your cost
for the plant and twice your cost for the container. Be prepared to
price any plant that you have out on rental, since you can easily
replace it.

When you see that your plant rental business is growing (no
pun intended) you will want to look into the prospects of obtaining a business loan so that you are able to expand. The Small

Business Administration offers financing in the form of a guaranteed loan, made possible with the participation of a bank.

You will be asked to provide a résumé of your business experience to date, which includes your personal background, present income and expenses, and a projection for the forthcoming year.

It's a good idea to contact your insurance agent to discuss your future needs. You will need fire insurance to cover your equipment and inventory. Liability insurance is especially important because you will be working with the public. You need to be protected against any lawsuits in case of damage to your customer's property while you are working there. If you have employees you need workman's compensation.

You will also need a running inventory to keep track of the plants and equipment you have out on rental, how long the plants have been rented and to whom, when they are to be picked up, and which plants need replacing.

17

SMALL FAMILY DAY CARE CENTER IN YOUR HOME

Here is a rich, rewarding experience for you—plus a way to earn money! All you will need is love, patience, and a home to do this in! A small family day care center is for you if you can provide this much-needed service. More and more mothers are working and the most important thing in their family life is finding someone who can provide warm and loving care for their children during the hours the mother works.

There are two ways to start a personal service like a day care center: One way is to do this yourself, using your own home and obtaining a license to provide this service.

Getting the approval for a small family day care center is the first step. The planning (zoning) department can conditionally approve the use of a single-family dwelling for the day care center. This is for a maximum of six children, including children who already live with you. For example, if you now have two children, then you can provide day care for a maximum of four children.

The other way of providing a day care center is to be a part of a network system of day care homes that are under the direction of a central agency. This is something like an association comprised of several family day care homes. This can also be a community action program. You will find the information you need for this in your phone book. This might be just the thing for you if you have never done anything like this before, so look into this before you make up your mind. The central agency to which you belong gives you all the help that you need to get started. If you decide to do this, then you will be working for the agency, not for yourself. They will pay you a salary instead of you collecting your own fees from the families.

Before you apply for your license, go to the doctor, as you will need him or her to fill out a form showing the license department that you are in good physical and mental health. You will also need to have new or recent tuberculosis X-rays or skin tests for yourself and family members under the age of sixteen.

The public health or welfare department will send over an inspector to see if there are any hazards in the wiring and plumbing of your home.

You must make a decision in the beginning as to the time you wish to spend in a family day care program. Since this is going to take place in your home, it is important for you to decide if you're going to spend a half-day a week or up to five or six full days.

You must also decide what age group you'll care for. Many programs care for children from the ages of three to six. You might decide on caring for younger children—say, from six months on—or even from infancy—this way you could keep them longer.

There is a large home-based group designed for handicapped children that includes preschoolers. You might want to get involved in helping with special problems and hold classes for the deaf, blind, cerebral palsied, physically handicapped and mentally handicapped—either retarded or emotionally disturbed. For those who are qualified, there are programs funded to hold classes for instructions in preprimary groups.

In most states the licensing or registrations are free, and you can go in at any time to fill out your application. The time you start to the time that you finish with the inspections shouldn't be more than a month. You can also receive from your state offices, free of charge, the many services they offer. Services include providing your name (after you qualify and are prepared) to persons who want day care for their children. They can also provide your day care home with play ideas, nutritional help, information on issues concerning day care routines, and new courses that will keep you current. There will be help everywhere for you—you won't have to go it alone! This is a public service, and, just like any other service, it is controlled by the state and its regulations, which insures that care of these children is according to the rules.

Here are some of the conditions that have to be met:

1. Fill out the forms provided by the agency, together with the fee required, for a *quasi-home* occupation permit. This is essentially a public service that is rendered in a private home.

2. If you live in an area that is located within 100 feet of your neighbor, you will probably be required to obtain the signatures of your neighbors indicating that they have no objection to your plans. If your neighbors have small children they will be delighted to have a small day care center in their midst!

LICENSING

Many people are surprised that caring for small children in your home would require a license. The reason is that day care is considered to be such an important factor in the welfare of children of all ages. These minimum requirements are intended to prevent all health and safety hazards from existing in or around your home. The agency also wishes to make sure that children in day care are not harmed physically or emotionally, and that they have a chance to grow and develop as they should in a healthy way.

In most states, the Department of Public Welfare has the responsibility for licensing. In some states licensing is done by the Department of Public Health, and in a few states this is done by special offices that coordinate children's services (The Massachusettes Office for Children and the Vermont Office of Child Development). All of these offices can license day care homes.

18

YOUR HOUSE OR APARTMENT—
HOW EXTRA SPACE
MEANS EXTRA MONEY

Many of us, because of low rent or old friendships, are living in quarters that are really too big for our retired needs. If you have an extra bedroom, go in and take a good look at it. It can be making extra money for you!

Yes, rent that extra space! But first think carefully. Ask yourself: What kind of person am I? Can I give up a large degree of privacy in order to have extra money? Before you decide, think *how* to rent. You have a choice:

1. *Rentals to share*: Sharing, to a senior woman, usually means renting to someone retired, someone who will cook, shop, and clean with you. You may even have meals together. You are both independent but share common interests and are compatible. The sharer pays half the rent and half or quarter for utilities.

2. *Room to rent*: You rent out only the room. The renter may be a student or businessperson, someone who is out all day and returns only to sleep. You might give privileges that include a quick breakfast or snack at odd hours. You give one shelf in the refrigerator and one in the cupboard for snacks. You decide if there will be cooking privileges. You furnish the bed linens laundered and the renter borrows your vacuum to clean the rented room.

The kind of person you are will determine how you advertise. Your ad will look something like this under "Rooms to Rent":

Furnished room, employed mature female (male), linens furnished, nonsmoker (?), on bus line (?), your phone number.

The neighborhood you live in will determine the weekly rate. When the renter calls, have the price ready and the following questions to ask:

1. Where is the person employed?
2. What is the person's previous residence? How long was he or she there?
3. Is the person a smoker or a nonsmoker?
4. Will the person bring a TV or radio? Discuss the use.
5. Can the person give you two references? Say that they will be checked (and then follow up).

If possible, have a friend or neighbor present at the appointment time to show the room. If you are in doubt about accepting the caller as a renter, take the phone number and say you will call back to make an appointment.

HOW TO DETERMINE THE WEEKLY RATE

1. Divide your monthly rent by 16 for the weekly rate. It can be raised or lowered according to privileges or disadvantages. If you find the seemingly right person, talk it over and reach an agreement before taking a deposit.
2. If you own or rent a condo, consult the management.
3. If you own your own home, ask around the neighborhood. You may prefer to use a rental agent (look in the Yellow Pages) who will screen applicants for you. Discuss fees.

SOME PITFALLS

1. You or the renter may be unhappy with the arrangement. Take one week's deposit in advance for a room to rent and one month in advance for sharing. If you're really unhappy at

the end of the specific time, say goodbye and find someone else.

2. If you must share a bathroom, you may be inconvenienced.

3. You and the renter may not be equally neat, especially in the kitchen. Try for an agreement!

4. Be sure you agree on smoking. If you smoke, find a smoker to rent to.

Note: Take a good look at the bedroom you are renting. It should have the following:

1. A bed with a comfortable mattress with protective cover, one or two good pillows with protective covers, two blankets, and a washable bedspread.

2. A writing table and straight chair with lamp.

3. A bedside reading table with lamp.

4. A comfortable easy chair.

5. A working window shade for light control.

YOUR HOUSE IS YOUR CASTLE!

Yes, if you own your own home, it is your castle. It may also be your burden—as the European nobility have discovered!

So what are they doing? They rent rooms to tourists, turn a wing into a hotel or restaurant, charge fees for castle tours—just to keep up with taxes, maintenance, inflation. There is no social stigma today to making your one real asset work for you.

If your house is too big for you, consider making a separate rental wing as an apartment. Probably you can do it—but there is one regulation that can stop you. Zoning!

To start:

1. Check the zoning of your neighborhood. If there are already two-family houses on your street, go ahead and plan. But if you are in a single family area (R1—meaning one resident family) do the following:

    a. In a small town consult the town fathers (mayor, town planner, council, etc.) A senior woman will usually be allowed to alter her house to fit her needs but may be asked to remove the second kitchen fixtures if she ever sells.

   b. In a city, ask for a zoning variance. This may be complicated and time-consuming. If, however, you have a relative who needs to be near you and will pay you rent, no variance is needed. It is simple to install a small kitchen unit back to back with already installed water, gas, or electric lines. Any plumber can do it.

2. Call in a plumber. Explain what you want to do and let him examine the present plumbing for an estimate. You can install anything from a glorious kitchen to an inexpensive, compact unit containing a stove, sink, and refrigerator. With luck, you already have a second bathroom for the rental. If not, get that estimate. Your plumber, contractor or appliance store can show you anything from the most luxurious to the most simple.

3. Now call in two more plumbers and get two more estimates and construction ideas.

Note: It will be less costly to keep your single-family meters. You can later work out a rental fee that covers the utilities. The fewer changes in wiring, the less the cost!

Entrance

If possible, remove a window and replace it with a convenient entrance door. A separate entrance will command a higher rental and you will enjoy the privacy. If you have a two-story house, do not attempt an outside stairway. Keep your present arrangement but install a wall or door to form an entrance hall. Again, the less construction, the lower the cost.

You now have three estimates and plans and can now proceed to the next step. How can you pay for your money-making rental?

1. The cheapest way is from a savings account. If you have a savings account, withdraw the necessary amount as the bills become due. Later, repay yourself a fixed amount each month from the rent you receive. You are paying no interest charges.

2. The next cheapest way is a collateral loan. Armed with your plans and estimates, talk to your banker. Using your savings

account as collateral, he or she will loan you the money with interest. However, the interest cost will be only the difference between the 5 ¼% interest on your savings account and the cost percent of the loan.

3. Home improvement loan: Again talk to your bankers, show them your plans and estimates. Go prepared to discuss the equity you have built up in your home, your present income, and any outstanding debts such as time payments.

4. Get a cosigner: A family member or friend with a good credit rating can agree to cosign with you. The bank will then consider the cosigner responsible for the loan, should you fail to pay.

5. Personal loan: Family or friend may loan you the money (probably with interest), knowing that you can repay a monthly percentage of the rental. If you calculate the share of the rent you can give the lender each month to reduce the loan, you have a businesslike offer to make.

Reminder: To a bank, a financing institution, a family member, or friend lending you money, there are just two important questions:

1. *Can* she pay it back?
2. *Will* she pay it back?

It is up to you to convince the lender. And then, on to those rental dollars!

19

PROPERTY MANAGEMENT— FREE TIME IS PROFIT!

Most managers of rental properties are women who got into the business through circumstances instead of long-range planning. Some women were renting their apartment in a complex, and out of boredom started helping the managers in looking after a vacant apartment. After months of showing apartments when the manager was gone on a vacation or shopping, women found that they liked this type of involvement with people. This is a very personal and rewarding profession. Working with the very large renting public might be right up your alley if you are outgoing, friendly, and assertive. This career has no age limit and can be done on a part-time or full-time basis.

Rental units come in all shapes and sizes—home, duplex, triplex, fourplex, and up. In the state of California units of sixteen or larger require a property manager who lives on the property, that is, a resident manager. Most resident managers are couples who work as a team, the woman takes care of the office work and rents the apartments, and the man takes care of the repairs and the exterior of the building.

Preparation is the key in starting any business venture. Public libraries have fine books that you can check to bring home and study. A few of these are recommended at the end of this chapter. Most banks and savings and loan institutions will give you free literature for starting your property management career. All you have to do is to request it. Your government's Small Business Administration will also furnish you with literature. If you do not have transportation, call the office and request that they mail it to you.

Special guidelines help you become more proficient in your management abilities. You will learn simple strategies to strengthen your self-confidence and make you project yourself in a more convincing manner. You will learn housing codes, keeping records, how to show an apartment, pricing the unit, lease/option agreements, screening tenants, taking deposits, making out inventory checklists, and more.

There is a lot of free help available for you. Property management is one of the courses given by most city colleges, and there are evening courses. Apartment owners associations have seminars during the day. These seminars are usually group meetings where problems are aired. You can ask questions about specific problems. There are many other benefits also for you. A legal service is usually available. Ask your stationery store owner about discounts for the many supplies it takes to manage units, no matter how small, such as credit statements, lease forms, deposit books and more.

Women who manage small rental units say their relationships with their owners are more like partnerships than boss/employee ones. Income property owners come from many different walks of life. Many owners are professional people who look upon their investment as a way to shelter their tax dollars. Young investing couples need someone to take good care of their units if they both hold full-time jobs. A lot of income properties are owned by investors who live out of town. The very largest percentage, however, consists of investors who fully intended to take care of their property in their spare time. Unfortunately, they have underestimated the time it takes to properly take care of rentals! The owners soon realize that poorly managed units not only decrease in value, but will decrease in equity if they are sold.

Women who prepare for this new career and professionals who want to update their knowledge take continuing education courses in property management. If you are just starting out or thinking about a career in this field, here are some simplified helpful rules to help you until you finish a few courses.

HOW MUCH IS THE RENT?

Owners of brand-new units want the rentals to cover the expenses plus the mortgage payments. First, you need to know how much a comparable unit is renting for in your same area and the surrounding areas. Check the local newspapers. Call on the ads that sound similar to what you have. Pretend that your are a prospective tenant and look at the rental to see what they have to offer compared to yours. The rents charged differ for the amenities that the apartments have. An apartment with a view will bring a better price than one whose windows overlook the alley. Smaller units rent faster than larger ones.

Some states have rent-control laws that prohibit rent increases. Property owners oppose this law because it limits the growth of new units, and, they believe, it discourages the banks from making them any new apartment loans. Call your local Apartment Owners Association to find out what the laws are in your state.

Use caution in raising the rents too frequently. This can cause tenants to move out. Too many vacant apartments at a time will give your owners not only a headache but a pain in the wallet to boot. Remember—keeping a good tenant is a lot better than trying to find a new one.

SHOWING THE APARTMENT

Showing an available apartment to a prospective tenant is no different from selling any product. Put your best smile forward—the more congenial you are, the less selling you will have to do.

First impressions are most important. The apartment must be clean if you wish to point out its best features. A view is a definite plus, so is ample closet space, a fireplace and a modern kitchen (most women will look at this first). If the couple has children, point out the close proximity to the schools (if there is are any).

While you are showing the apartment to the prospective tenants, start asking them questions about themselves. You will be expected to weed out the undesirable tenant, but remember that federal laws prohibit discrimination of race, religion, sex, or origin. Before you start renting any apartment study the discrimination laws. Undesirable tenants may know their rights (and you should always assume that they do). If you refuse to rent them an apartment because you have a "gut" feeling that they are not right for the apartment, and give an excuse that the apartment is already rented, you could find yourself facing a lawsuit in a state or federal court.

You can, however, qualify the tenants on the basis of their income, on the size of their family (if you have a one-bedroom apartment to rent and the couple has two or three children, you can refuse to rent) and pets. The best way to handle all this is to have them fill out an application. It should include the following information:

1. Names of husband, wife, number of children and their ages, pets.
2. The social security numbers of both parties.
3. Driver's license numbers of both parties. (This is an excellent way to find them if they skip out on you.)
4. Previous address, how long they lived there, and reasons for leaving.
5. References: personal, business, and two relatives.
6. Place of employment, length of time there, and the telephone number.
7. Permission for a credit report. (The tenant pays for this one.)

If the credit report comes back looking good and you have carefully checked on the rest of the information, you have done all that you can in insuring yourself a good tenant.

LEASES

Standard lease forms are available in any stationery store. Apartment owners associations have better-prepared leases. An oral agreement between parties is legal; however, a written lease signed by both parties is much preferred.

A month-to-month lease is renewed each month. Tenants must give thirty days' notice if they wish to move out, and you must give thirty days' notice if you wish to raise the rent.

A six-month lease guarantees that the rent will not be raised for six months. This is a term lease and does not require a thirty days' notice. If you wish to raise the rent, simply put the larger amount on the next lease.

A one-year or longer lease is the same as the six-month lease. If it has a clause that makes it a lease/option then you extend the lease at the same terms as the original lease. Tenants prefer this arrangement as it insures them the apartment without having to pay any more money.

A sublease is an arrangement the tenant makes for a substitute to occupy the apartment while they move out. As the lease with you is still in effect, this cannot be done without your approval. You will have to have an application and a credit statement from the sublessee just as you did with the original tenant.

LATE-PAYING TENANT

You have to get tough. Writing a letter to a tenant who makes a habit of paying late will not only do you no good but you will start a precedent and they will never pay you on time! A face-to-face confrontation immediately is necessary. Always write a late charge for overdue rents in the leases. This charge is usually from $3 to $10 for each day late. When tenants read this late charge clause in their lease they'll know you mean business. If you are lax you will be taken advantage of. Never let anyone move into the apartment until they have paid their first and last month's rent/security deposits. Renters sometimes are under the impression that if the rent is due on the first, they are not late if they pay up by the tenth—not so. If the rent is due on the first and they have not paid, start the late charges on the second. Send an eviction notice on the fifteenth. Stay with this procedure or you will be sorrier each month. Bad tenants will give you all kinds of excuses. Don't allow the tenants to give you their problems. Your owners do not wish to become "lenders!"

DEPOSITS

Before tenants move in any apartment, a whole array of deposits confront them. It is necessary that they have a clear understanding of what these deposits are for, what they can expect back when they move out, and what they will hate to forfeit. This information is written in the lease; however, as you receive the money, note it also on the deposit receipt.

Security Deposit

The security deposit is a security or guarantee that the tenant will not damage your apartment and will pay the rent when it comes due. While you are filling out the lease forms, make it clear that the security deposit is separate from the rental fee. The amount of the security deposit that you charge depends on the circumstances of the tenant. If the tenants have children, or if there are to be pets in the apartment, the security deposit should be at least one-half of the monthly rent. Make up a small checklist of the condition of the apartment before the tenants move in. Go over it with the tenants and have them sign it before they move in:

1. The apartment walls, stove, refrigerator, and the bathroom are clean and in good condition.
2. The rugs are clean and in good condition.
3. All the electrical appliances are in good working order.

If there are things that need repair, note the items on the bottom of the list also. All parties must sign these checklists, and if you think there might be any problems, take some pictures.

Key Deposits

A key deposit is usually about $6. This is based on four keys at $1.50 per key. You will find that most tenants lose the keys or sometimes just don't bother to turn them in when they leave.

Pet Deposit

A pet owned by an indifferent tenant can cause a lot more damage than the largest cleaning/security deposit. The only alternative that an owner has is to have a pet agreement between the tenants and the manager. The pet agreements are available from apartment owners associations for their members. Check periodically to see if the tenant has the same number of pets as when the original agreement was signed!

STANDARD MANAGEMENT FEES

Large complexes are almost always handled through professional management firms. They also do the hiring for their resident managers (these are the people you should contact when you have enough experience). They handle all of the records: daily records, depreciation schedules, loan and insurance records, expense records, maintenance records, and so on. Their monthly charge for these services is usually from 3 percent to 8 percent of the gross income. Resident managers usually receive part reduction in the rent and part salary.

The arrangements between a manager of small units (from four to eight units) and the owner differs. Sometimes it's more advantageous for the manager to have free rent. Your charge for managing the units will depend on the size of the units and/or how much work you will be required to do. For a fourplex that rents for $350 per month per unit, a standard fee for management would be 10 percent of the gross income. This would give you $140 a month, and you would be required to keep the apartments rented and give the owners a monthly statement of the income and expenses. A nonrefundable cleaning fee is usually about $35 to $50 and many women prefer to keep the cleaning fee by doing the work themselves.

Start now by looking for all the free preparatory courses you can get in the field of property management. If you live in an apartment now, contact the owner and tell him that you have prepared yourself for a career in property management. Offer to help rent the apartments as they become vacant. See if you can get yourself bonded. A bond is a form of insurance for the apartment owner, guaranteeing coverage if the manager steals any money. It's a standard practice. You will then be able to collect the rents and maybe work yourself into a free apartment. Even if you get a substantial reduction in your rent, it is no different from getting a small salary. If there is nothing at the place you live, place a small ad in the newspaper stating that you will take care of small units at a reasonable price. If you get more than you can handle, call a friend or two to help out. This is the way a lot of small businesses grow into large ones!

See these books for further information: *Income Expense and Analysis: Apartments, Condos and Co-ops* by Kenneth Anderson, *Institute of Real Estate Management* by Kenneth Anderson, and *Principles of Real Estate Management* by James Downs, Jr.

20

THE HANDCRAFTS BUSINESS: TURN A PART-TIME PLEASURE INTO A FULL-TIME JOB!

The interest in handcrafted items is growing by leaps and bounds. The public enjoys buying clever handcrafted items of quality in local gift shops, drugstores, and grocery stores.

The demand is for distinctive, individually crafted wares, and women who see this fast-growing trend are offering their own handcrafted items to this market.

Do you spend your leisure time happily working with clay, metal, wood, glass, leather, paper, or weaving, quilt-making, sewing, or basket-making?

Have you produced an item so distinctive that your family, your friends, and now friends of friends want to buy it?

If so, then you have probably been thinking that you would like to devote full time to making and selling your handcraft.

But first analyze yourself. Ask yourself the following:

1. Do I have another source of income for a few months, or even a year, to cover my living expenses and the necessary materials and production costs?

2. If I am accustomed to a regular job, could I stand the isolation and the self-supervision for craftwork?

3. Do I have the necessary knowledge and discipline to meet the deadlines and schedules of my commitments?

4. Having designed and made my product, do I have the energy and the confidence to go out and market it?

Since you already know you have a marketable product, then the last question is probably the most important. If you do not wish to market it yourself, try to find a friend or relative who can act as a business partner to do the market research for you. You'll need to know:

1. The size of the market, the best way to reach it, and the cost of reaching your potential buyers.
2. The potential profit to you after supplies and labor are calculated.
3. Compared to similar products, how your handcraft rates in durability, attractiveness, and affordability.
4. Any changeable conditions, such as climate or style, that might change the demand for your product.

PRODUCTION IN YOUR HOME

At this point, you are still working your craft at home.

Therefore, before beginning a production process or installing further equipment, you must consult your zoning and fire officials. You may need the correct fire extinguishers or need to upgrade your insurance policy.

EQUIPMENT AND MATERIALS

You probably have the necessary equipment to go into business. You can, however, make two mistakes—work with limited equipment that will hamper your flexibility and slow your growth, or rush out and buy equipment too large for your needs and incur unnecessary expense. Talk to equipment suppliers; if you cannot purchase new equipment, consider, at least for a start, buying used equipment or leasing from the supplier.

Your materials can be the major expense so you will have to find out the most economical means of purchasing. Try for discount percentages by consolidating small orders into one large one, or join up with other craftspeople whose needs are the same, in order to get the volume discounts.

Once you have a reliable source of supply, poster it so you will be kept up to date on new equipment and colors. Remember, however, that until you have achieved a credit standing, you must pay cash on delivery.

FINANCING

To start your handcraft business, you may need some financial assistance. You may plan to buy more equipment to pay for materials or to rent a studio in a permitted zoning area.

1. Start with family and friends who have confidence in your product.
2. You can take a second deed of trust on your home.
3. If you have a bank account, talk to your bank about a loan. Before your banker loans you money for a new handcraft business, you will have to provide an inventory of equipment and materials, permit expenses, and insurance payments.
4. In a small town, you must be refused by one bank, or in a town over 200,000, by two banks to qualify for a Small Business Administration loan. You yourself will be expected to put up 50 percent of the cost of the project but minority and economically disadvantaged groups have lower capital requirements. (See Index for details on SBA.)

GOVERNMENT ASSISTANCE

The government will send you free publications that provide technical and financial assistance. Write to:

Economics, Statistics and Cooperatives Services
U.S. Department of Agriculture, Washington, D.C. 20250
(A source of publications and workshops to help craftspeople learn the business for success.)

Information Staff
Farmers Home Administration
Department of Agriculture
Washington, D.C. 20250
(Have loan guarantee programs to assist craftspeople for community development activities.)

Science & Education Administration
U.S. Department of Agriculture
Washington, D.C. 20250
(To learn about activities at the local level.)

Information Office
National Endowment for the Arts
Washington, D.C. 20506
(Provides grants and programs guidelines.)

General Manager
The Indian Arts and Crafts Board
Department of the Interior
Washington, D.C. 20240
(Provides educational material and technical and financial assistance
programs for native American crafts projects.)

Small Business Administration
Washington, D.C. 20416
(Specify "Free Management Assistance Publications SBA 115-A" and "For
Sale Booklets SBA 114B".)

LOOKING AHEAD

In this section on handcrafters, we have assumed you are just
starting out and working alone. Perhaps, until now, you have only
a family member or friend to help you.

However, should you find that the volume is more than you
can handle and the orders too big to accept, you may need the
following:

Studio Help: In addition to the salary of anyone you hire, you
are responsible for social security taxes, worker's compensation,
and withholding taxes.

Sales Representative: Also called a sales agent or manufacturer's representative, this person can reach markets at a distance
and save you time for production. A written contract is important
because the sales representative works on commission—from 5
percent to 30 percent of the wholesale price—paid only after you
have been paid. To find a sales representative, ask a retailer or look
in your trade magazine.

HOW WILL YOU PRICE YOUR CRAFT?

Unless your product is extremely unique and without competition, you must know at what price other craftspeople are selling
similar products for. If you intend to fill orders to stores, calculate:

1. The fixed costs, or overhead, such as utilities, rent, and insurance.
2. The cost of raw materials and the dollar value of labor (your time and anyone working with you).

Added together, you have the wholesale price. The retail price set by a store is generally a 100 percent markup.

READY TO SELL?

You have built up an inventory of your product and are really ready to sell! You have several ways to go now:

Selling Wholesale

This means you sell to the stores by either a sales representative or yourself. Start with a few small stores in the nearby area. Most people shop at the same store for a particular type of merchandise. To reach these people, concentrate your efforts on the stores that likely customers will shop in. The right outlet for you will be the one whose clientele are able to buy and whose merchandise is of a similar quality. The owners are usually the buyers and they are also behind the counters selling their products.

It is a good idea to phone ahead for an appointment. Ask when it would be best for you to come in. They may have a "buying day" for would-be vendors to show their wares. When you are assembling your work in preparation for the appointment, take only a few samples that your are especially proud of. These will show the buyer the feeling you have for your work. Offer to leave photographs of the rest of your work with the store owner to look over when he or she is not rushed.

Be sure to work out a price list of the wholesale price to the retailer. Good business practice (and the law) requires the same price list to all of the outlets that will handle your crafts.

Selling on Consignment

You place your product in a retail store, but you get paid only after the article is sold. This is an excellent way to sell—in fact, many craftspeople who produce high quality products use consignment exclusively. There is a twofold benefit—you are able to get the exposure you need for your work free of charge and the retailer does not have to put money out in order to have merchandise to sell. However, deal only with an honest and well-capitalized merchant and keep accurate records, dates, and descriptions of your products left with each store.

If the store does not have a consignment form, obtain two from your stationery supply store and you can sign one. The store will get 30 percent or 50 percent of the selling price.

Selling Retail

You sell at retail price direct to the customer either from your home or at craft fairs. Selling directly to the customer may seem more attractive pricewise than selling wholesale, but you are spending time selling rather than producing. If your home or studio is on a busy street, just your sign will bring in the browsers. That is selling on a daily basis, but you may prefer to build up an inventory and exhibit at craft fairs.

CRAFT FAIRS AND ART SHOWS

Craft fairs and art shows could be the outlet for you!

The kind of craft show you exhibit at depends on your locale and how far you are willing to travel—anything from a small church fair to a city-sponsored art festival! But however small the show, you will reach the retail market and the public will get to know you. You may even meet buyers or wholesalers looking for new items. For the craftsperson who works at home and has a limited inventory, the small shows and fairs are excellent.

Small Shows

Here you can talk to people, give out your business cards, obtain names for mailing lists, and invite the local folks to see your studio. Small shows are fun as well as profitable! And be sure to look into the local flea markets—some towns have a weekly flea market.

Large and Sophisticated Shows

The large shows have the following drawbacks:

1. You may have to consider travel costs and lodging costs (tax deductible).

2. You may be required to attend your display yourself, sales-people not permitted.

3. You may need to purchase display tables and panels not pro-vided by the exhibit.

4. You will probably have to pay an entry fee ranging from $25 to $100 to the show sponsors. Or you may be asked to pay 5 per-cent to 30 percent on what you take in on your sales.

5. Some shows require that you be *juried*—that is, you must qualify for showing by submitting your work by sample or slides to the sponsor.

Attend a large craft show, see how it operates, and get the name of the organizer from the exhibitors. Then send a letter to the organizer after the show expressing your interest and asking for the entry requirements for the next show. If you feel your art is worth surmounting the difficulties, go for the recognition as well as the money!

STREET EXHIBITS

Exhibiting at street exhibitions could be the outlet for you!

Many craftspeople have discovered that the street can be a regular source of income—in fact, in cities that require a license there are long lists for street-selling spaces.

With the right climate and the right neighborhood, men and women, young and old, all with talent, are showing their products to street customers. Some cities and parks have art commission or recreation departments to promote street exhibits, especially to encourage tourism.

Some craftspeople work at the exhibit to save time, attract the curious, and of course, the buyers.

However, be sure to check the local regulations. The police department or sheriff's office can tell you where to inquire to clear local ordinances or to obtain a license.

Then join the many clever artisans who are finding money on the street!

21

HOW YOU CAN TEACH SEWING

If you are a skilled seamstress—with years of experience in cutting patterns and stitching seams—now is the time for you to begin teaching the seven out of eight young women who are now turning to home sewing.

Even affluent women are looking for instruction in creating smart, individual, *economical* fashions. "I made it myself" is no longer said apologetically—it is said with pride.

Most sewing classes are offered in department, fabric, or sewing machine stores for high fees but with little individual attention. Young or working women cannot always attend scheduled classes, so that a convenient appointment with an experienced teacher in her own home is a boon to the ambitious—but inexperienced—sewer.

HOW TO FIND YOUR STUDENTS

Rural Areas

Advertise by word of mouth and by placing notices on church, club, and grocery store bulletin boards. You can put a small ad in the local newspaper—perhaps the editor will give you a write-up. If you live within a reasonable distance from a fabric shop, let the owner know you are giving lessons in dressmaking. He will sell more fabric if he can recommend you for lessons or for dressmaking to his customers.

If you are far from a fabric center you can stock and sell piece goods as well as teach sewing. Your area and climate will determine the type of material you sell. You may find yourself stocking patterns, remnants, sewing supplies—and soon have a mini-center in your own home. With no overhead and no competition, your small investment in a stock of sewing-related items would have a potential.

City and Mall Areas

Obtain your students by word of mouth, printed cards, local ads, bulletin boards, and referrals from fabric stores. Department stores with large fabric departments usually hold their own scheduled sewing classes. Small department stores may be willing to post a notice of your private lessons in the fabric department.

If you can teach tailoring, lining, zipper placement, buttonholing, and the like, you can advance the beginner beyond the basics and keep her coming for fittings. In the city, stress the selection of good fabric because the price will seem reasonable compared to the dress just seen in a couture shop.

The owner of your large city fabric shop has trade pressure and fierce competition. If the owner can recommend you to the young marrieds, teenagers, and even men who want to create economical, well-fitted garments, he or she will sell more yardage. If you are an experienced sewer, you are a gift to the industry of home sewing!

HOW MUCH TO CHARGE

A sewing course is usually scheduled for eight two-hour lessons. An instructor of a class of six or eight students receives $10 or more an hour as part of the store's fabric promotion. However, in a rural area where baby sitters get only about $1 per hour, you would charge about $2 per hour. In a city area where baby sitters get $2 or $3 per hour, you can charge more. Your area will determine your fee.

Plan the course and explain the time involved in each step. Teach the best way first, later the shortcuts. It takes a skilled operator to run up a seam without first basting!

After lessons in dressmaking for beginners, you can offer tailoring, pattern adjusting, and construction of swimsuits and ski suits, children's jackets and coats, and men's wear.

A new trend in home sewing is bedspreads and curtains. Pattern companies are now promoting patterns and instruction books for making placemats, draperies, sleeping bags, table covers, and more. If you decide to sell fabrics, you can sell an order up to fifteen yards or more for home decorating—and even instruct how to make a housecoat to match!

TRENDS

It is projected that about 40 percent to 50 percent more people will be sewing at home in the next five years. The younger generation will expand the fabric centers and dressmaking demand. The small shop, the mom-and-pop store, may not survive, but the large fabric centers should succeed. The home-based instructor (you!) should capture a share of the home sewing market.

HINTS ON PAMPERING YOUR STUDENTS

1. Hang a bulletin board for the display of fashions and fashion events.
2. Arrange a "kiddie kage"—a play pen or fenced-in area for the small children of mothers who must bring them along.
3. Talk to the teacher of home economics in your high school—you can offer discounts to her and her students and she can guide you on youthful trends.
4. If you like public speaking, talk to clubs, churches, and schools on the advantages of home sewing, its techniques and choices.

The following associations can help you:

American Home Sewing Council, Inc.
40 East 38th Street
New York, NY 10016
Publication: "Selling Home Sewing"

Textile Association of Los Angeles
819 Santee Street
Los Angeles, CA 90014
Publication on materials: "Tala West Coast Retail Directory"

The following periodicals can help you:

Home Sewing Trade News
129 Broadway
Lynbrook, NY 11563

Sew Business
1271 Avenue of Americas, Suite 3560
New York, NY 10020

22

HOW TO TEACH NEEDLECRAFT

Instead of home sewing, you may prefer to teach needlecraft!

If you are experienced in any one or all of the following crafts you can offer a real service to beginners: knitting, crocheting, needlepoint, embroidery, or rug making. Not only must a beginner learn the technique of the stitches, but she must learn to interpret patterns. Sweaters must be knitted to size, afghans must be crocheted to pattern, needlepoint stitched or created artistically, and rugs to last. Without help, the beginner falters and gives up.

The information in the preceding pages on home sewing also pertains to teaching needlecraft. Visit your local yarn shop and learn if they give their own lessons. If they will refer their customers to you, they will save time and sell more yarn. Be prepared with cards or posters.

For needlecrafting, a small group can be scheduled in your own home over a cup of coffee. Needlecraft is a sociable occupation and you will find a few friends coming together to your lessons, not only to learn but to chat!

If your community is distant from yarn supplies, consider investing in a display of yarns and related items such as knitting needles, crochet hooks, pattern books, and patterns. Check with your local chamber of commerce concerning permits for selling in your own home. Because states and townships vary in retailing requirements and zoning, any large undertaking requires checking the laws.

HOW TO PAMPER YOUR NEEDLECRAFTERS

1. Provide adequate lighting.
2. Provide a "kiddie kage" with toys for the small child who must accompany his mother.
3. Have a coffee tray set up with disposable cups.
4. Casually display some of your own expert craft handiwork.

For information:

> National Notions Association
> 350 Fifth Ave., Suite 1309
> New York, NY 10001
>
> California Needlework Association
> 2165 Jackson Street
> San Francisco, CA 94415

23

DISCOUNT CLOTHES FOR CHILDREN

In a little shop or in your own home you can sell children's clothes at half price to thrifty mothers. If you live within travel distance of a big city wholesale clothing market, you can buy the merchandise as low as one-half the wholesale price by paying cash.

Example: A dress that retails at $15 costs $8 wholesale. For cash, the manufacturer discounts from a backlog of clothing, and you pay $4. You can then sell for $8 an item worth twice as much to delighted customers.

You will find many manufacturers of children's clothing in the phone book. Make an appointment with the manufacturer and take your cash. You will be shown what is called "off sizes." An off size means that if, say, the manufacturer is making girls' dresses between the sizes of 6X and 14, there may be sizes not heavily ordered by a retail store. These become the backlog on the manufacturer's discount rack, and you, for cash, could get another one-half off! You then fill in with the few sizes at the regular wholesale price. Your profits should be more than 100 percent.

If you plan to rent a storefront, you will need a business license from city hall. The mannequins used for display in your store or in your home, can be inexpensively made by a wrought iron company or a wire products manufacturing firm in your area.

Because this is a "cash and carry" business, you will need a station wagon to transfer between your wholesale manufacturer and your "Thrifty Miss" shop!

TWO PIECES.
ROD INSERTS INTO
THE BASE.

III

Before You Send for the Repairman . . .

TELEVISION

Check all the channels. Check with your neighbor. The problem may be in the station, not your television set. Ghosts or double images could appear because the antenna wire in the cable is disconnected. Or your outside antenna may be turned by the wind.

Check to make sure the plug is in. Try the set on another plug to see if the socket is faulty.

Never set liquid or plants to be watered on top of your TV—you can cause a short. And because of corrosion, keep the window closed behind the television, especially if you live near the ocean.

NEVER open the back of your television yourself, even though unplugged. There can be stored electrical power in certain parts.

REFRIGERATOR

If your refrigerator does not run, open the door to see if the light is working. If the light is off, check your circuit breaker or fuse box. You may have overloaded the wire with another appliance.

Strange noises? Check the defrost pan and all dishes and bottles that may be rattling together.

Check your freezer to make sure the door is closing properly. Older refrigerators can build up ice or slide food forward. Check the shelves for the right position so that doors seal properly.

Never use a lamp extension cord. A refrigerator must have a heavy duty cord or you can get a burned-out compressor.

Avoid placing food tightly against the refrigerator walls. Allow for circulation of air around the food.

GAS STOVE

If the burner does not light, check the burner holes and the pilot light hole to see if they are plugged.

Do not use aluminum foil on the rack under baking pans or on an oven bottom. It changes heat flow improperly.

Flat-bottom pans cook better and save energy.

Stagger pans on two racks so heat flows easily.

Allow the oven to reach the desired temperature before placing pans in the oven and do not crowd.

ELECTRIC RANGE

If the oven and broiler does not work, check the automatic clock. Put it back on manual. You may have accidentally turned it on while cleaning.

If one part of stove works but not another, check the circuit breakers. One side of the breaker could be tripped. The circuit breaker is usually found in a hall closet (a small door in a wall at eye level). In older houses, the fuse box is in the cellar and you simply check or replace the fuse.

Surface units not heating? The element may not be plugged in, or the electric receptical it plugs into may be out of adjustment. Turn off the circuit breaker to the range, then adjust the receptical. If the element does not work after you turn on the power, it may need replacing. Take it to the service agency and have it tested.

If you line the drip pan under your electric burner with foil, cut a hole in the center of the foil. The hole in the center of the drip pan is a vent. If you cover that vent, the wires will overheat.

TENDER LOVING CARE FOR YOUR CAR

Most of the gas stations throughout the country have cut down on the help and are geared for a self-service operation. Many of us know absolutely nothing about servicing our car, and this is a terrible state of affairs. We do know, however, that neglecting our car's maintenance invites both disaster and high repair bills, both of which we wish to avoid.

How do we get the lower price of self-service gas and still take care of our car at the same time? We *can* do the things a service station attendant did for us by doing the maintenance at home. Here are some step-by-step procedures for those who have never even looked under the hood, or never knew what we were looking at.

How to Lift the Hood

Release the handle on the inside of your car. Facing the hood, carefully slide your fingers in the small opening under the hood until you find a metal catch that you can press *up*. While lifting the hood you will see in front of you a long metal bar that is used to prop up the hood. Lift this bar and hook it securely into the slot on the underside of the hood. You are now ready to start.

Checking the Motor Oil

Use a flashlight and look down into the middle of the car, then left or right, until you find a metal loop. Hook your finger around the loop and pull it up. This is called a dipstick and is used to find out how much oil you still have in the motor (a white baggie tie will make it easier to find the next time). Wipe it clean with a rag and reinsert it making sure you push it all the way in for an accurate reading. Pull the dipstick out again. The oil level is correct if it is between the "max" and "min" marks. The difference between the two marks is about one quart. If you need a quart of oil, open the large metal cap to the *motor* and pour the oil.

Caution: Sometimes the cap to the motor and the cap to the radiator look the same, so before you pour any oil, test the fluid with your fingertip. If the liquid is brown, you've found the motor.

If you drive on only short trips, the engine oil should be changed every 3,000 miles. If your driving is mostly on longer trips, the oil should be changed every 6,000 miles. For owners of diesel cars, your oil must be changed after each severe driving session, because the engine oil can become diluted with diesel fuel; the oil will become too thin, and this could damage the parts. You should also use an additive (ask your mechanic which is best for your car) to the oil, which keeps the car's motor clean and running more smoothly.

Checking the Radiator

Never open the radiator if the engine is hot! When the engine is cold, remove the large metal cap that covers the radiator and look inside. The color of the fluid could be green or blue, and is not to be confused with motor oil. The color comes from the coolant, and the radiator should contain equal parts of coolant and water. The fluid level must be checked each fall, because the hot summer weather causes the fluids to evaporate and lose their protective properties. Check the fluid level more often during the summer, especially if your car has a tendency to overheat. If the radiator ever gets dark brown inside or you find rust around the throat, have the radiator system flushed out and add fresh coolant. Make sure the radiator fluid covers the vertical radiator pipes at all times.

Checking the Tires

If your tire pressure is not checked regularly, abnormal wear can occur. By simply correcting underinflated tires, you can improve your mileage! The only tool that you need to check your own tires is a tire gauge. This is an inexpensive tool that looks like a ballpoint pen. To use it, first untwist the cap on the tire's air valve; then place the blunt end of the gauge squarely over the air valve. The other end has a hidden pressure scale that comes out of the bottom (the smaller end) at the same time. This reading of the scale tells you how much air you have in the tire. Your owner's manual will tell you the proper pressure for your tires. If you need air, drive over to the air hose at the service station and put air in the tire. Recheck the air to find the pressure. Put the cap back on the valve and repeat this procedure for the other three tires.

If you are planning to care for your car and need more information, auto repair manuals are usually available for less than $10. Before you buy a manual, decide on what you want to do for your car and check the manual to see if it has what you need to know. If you want to change the oil, choose tires, or find out how your brake system works, buy a general manual. Should you wish to do more serious repair work there are manuals for your make of car. Beginning repair books have lots of pictures and are divided into specific chapters on tires, the electrical system, and so on. A good book should also have an index for easy reference.

Checking the Battery

The battery is located under the hood. It looks like a large black box and has usually six white caps on its top, which would be a standard twelve-volt battery. The battery should be checked often. And because of the acid in the battery it's best to wear rubber gloves when checking it. Unscrew the caps and look inside. You will see a transparent cell with a lower and upper mark. If the fluid is below the lower mark fill it up with distilled water. *Never* fill water past the upper mark or the acid will overflow when the battery is charged, causing damage to the battery. The fluid level in each cell should always be between the upper and lower marks.

How often you need to add water (distilled only) depends mainly on how much driving you are doing and how the weather conditions are. Usually the water level is checked more often in the hot summer months or before and after long trips. When the weather gets colder, however, your battery will get weaker. A battery that is used in normal weather gives its full power, but it operates at about 75 percent at freezing and 40 percent at zero degrees.

Look at your battery and see if it looks corroded around the terminals (this is where the electrical cables are hooked). If it looks bad, take it to the service station to have it cleaned. If not, buy a can of silicone spray to keep rust and corrosion away. On a really cold day this corrosion could mean the difference between starting and not starting. Your battery needs all the help it can get.

If you smoke, put out your cigarette before you work around the battery. Hydrogen gas is emitted by a battery and is explosive, so be very careful. Remove hanging necklaces and your wristwatch to avoid any electrical contact while you are checking the water level.

Jump-Starting a Battery

If jump-starting your dead battery from another car's good battery is ever necessary, here is a simple procedure that will get you going in no time flat. Before you start, however, there are some precautions that you *must* follow:

1. Thaw a frozen battery first before you connect the battery cables. (Your battery is frozen if there is ice in its fluid.) Check for corrosion on the battery terminals, because it will reduce the amount of current flow from your battery by half. Batteries lose power in cold weather.
2. Remove jewelry and wristwatch.
3. Do not lean over the battery.
4. Remove the caps from the water cells and put a wet cloth over the openings. (Discard the cloth after use.)
5. Turn off everything in your car. The other car must be running.
6. Both batteries must be the same voltage. Check by counting the caps from the water cells; they must be identical.
7. Make sure the vehicles are *not* touching.
8. Apply the emergency brakes and put the car in neutral. Take out the keys and set your parking brakes.

Look at your battery where the electrical connections are and you will find one *plus* and one *minus* sign in the back of each terminal. You must first attach one end of the positive (+) cable to the positive terminal of the good battery. Then attach the other end of the positive cable to the positive terminal of the dead battery. Take the negative (−) cable and attach one end to the negative terminal of the good battery. The other end of the negative cable should be grounded by attaching it to the engine block of the nonstarting car. Now start your engine.

To remove the cables, reverse the order in which you put them on, being careful to avoid moving parts.

Never push or tow a car with a catalytic converter or damage to other parts may result.

IV
The Government: How It Can Save You Money, How It Can Make You Money

24

TELESERVICE

Did you know that the U.S. Department of Health and Human Services has a special telephone service that you can use simply by calling your local social security office?

You can use this service to get information on almost anything concerning questions or services provided by HHS.

You can use it to:

a. Apply for social security or supplemental security income payments. You may not be able to complete your claim by phone, but you can get it started.

b. Apply for Medicare.

c. Find out how to change your name or address on your records.

d. Report a change in your marital status.

e. Report that you have stopped or started work or other changes that could affect your payments.

f. Report a lost or stolen check or a delayed payment.

g. Find out how to replace a lost or missing social security or Medicare card.

h. Get assistance with filling out your Medicare claim forms.

i. Get information about direct deposit of your checks.

j. Get an estimate of your monthly benefit amount.

k. Request a statement of your earnings record.

l. Find out whether a particular health facility participates in Medicare.

m. Get help in requesting a review of the decision made on your claim.

Your local social security representative will also help you get general information or publications about social security, supplemental security income, and Medicare.

Note: If your call concerns your benefit checks, be sure to give your social security claim number, which is shown on your check. If you are calling about Medicare have your card handy.

25

SOCIAL SECURITY

QUESTIONS AND ANSWERS

Q: Will I lose my social security benefits if I work?

A: If you are 65 years of age or older, you can earn up to $6,960 in 1984 and not lose any benefits. If you are between the ages of 62 and 65, you can earn up to $5,160 in 1984 without losing any benefits.

Q: What will happen to my benefits if I make over this limit?

A: When your earnings go over the amount that you can earn for the year, the Social Security Administration will deduct $1 for each $2 you have earned over the allotted amount. For example, if you are 65 years of age and are now receiving a monthly benefit of $400, you could earn $16,560 in 1984 before *all* of your benefits were withheld. You must count all of your earnings for the whole year in figuring the benefits due you. For most people, this means January through December. You will be required to file an income tax return by April of the following year. Those 70 and older will be able to earn as much as possible without losing any of their present benefits.

Q: What does the Social Security Administration mean by earnings?

A: If you are working for somebody else, count all of your yearly gross income, the amount you received before deductions. If you are paid partly in cash and partly in some other form, such as meals or living quarters, include both the cash and the value of the other form of payment in figuring your total earnings. Domestics and farm workers count the cash wages. They do not have to count the room and board. Commissioned employees shoud know that social security is interested in the time period that your money was earned, not when it was paid to you. This includes commissions and profit sharing.

Any and all increases in your wage base will be reflected in future higher benefits for you. The more you pay into social security, the more you will receive in your monthly check when you retire. The monthly amount of social security benefits you are entitled to is based on the average earnings you received while you were working.

Q: Will the income from my investments reduce the benefits I am now getting from social security?

A: The only change that reduces the benefits you are now receiving is earned income that comes from your employment or self-employment. Here are some other types of income that you can receive *without reducing your benefits:*

    a. Interest on savings accounts.

    b. Income from pensions or other types of retirement pay.

    c. Income from annuities.

    d. Income or shares of income you receive as a limited partner from a trade or business.

    e. Gain or loss from the sale of capital assets (stocks, real estate, etc.).

    f. Gifts or inheritances.

    g. Rental income from real estate (unless you are a real estate dealer).

    h. Interest or dividends from stocks and bonds (unless you are a stock broker).

    i. Royalties you received in or after the year that you became 65 from patents or copyrights that you had before the year of your retirement.

    j. Sick pay if it started six months or more after you left the employment.

    k. Pay for jury duty.

    l. Loans received by employees—unless you repaid it by work.

    m. Worker's compensation.

    n. Prize winnings from contests (unless it is your trade or business).

o. Tips less than $20 a month, or tips that are not paid in cash.

p. Any income from employment or self-employment that you earned in or after you became 70, starting in January of 1983.

Q: I am self-employed and won't know how much I will make this year. How do I count my earnings?

A: Count all of your *net* earnings if you are self-employed. The main consideration is whether you are active in your business and are performing "substantial services."

The Social Security Administration does not use a monthly earnings system for self-employed persons. They look at the amount of *time* that you devote to your business, the kinds of services that you perform, and how many hours you actually work.

If you work more than forty-five hours in a month your services are considered substantial. If you work fewer than forty-five hours a week, your services may be considered substantial if *you are in a management position*. If you work fewer than fifteen hours in any one month, your services are *never* considered substantial regardless of the size or value of the business. In other words, self-employed persons *can* get their same benefits if they do not perform substantial services.

Q: I'm over 65 years old and will make more than the $6,960 limit this year. Will I lose my Medicare benefits along with part of my social security?

A: You will never lose your Medicare benefits—no matter how much income you earn.

Q: What happens to social security benefits when a retired worker wants to go back to work?

A: If you are now receiving benefits checks, your total family benefits may be affected because of your additional earnings, because social security will withhold all or part of your benefits. Happily, though, when you return to work after you start getting your retirement checks, your added earnings will result in higher benefits in the future. Social Security will automatically refigure your benefits after the additional earnings are credited to your account.

Q: Will alimony payments affect my social security?
A: No.

Q: How do workers qualify for social security?
A: By working for at least ten years. Each year that you have

worked earn you credits. You can get the present status of your earnings at any time from your local Social Security office. If you stopped working before you were entitled to retirement benefits, the credits stay on your record and you can add to it at any time by going back to work in a job covered by social security.

Q: How long after I apply will I get my first check?

A: It usually takes about sixty days for the checks to start coming. There is a special procedure, however, that speeds up the processing of your claim to twenty days instead of the normal sixty days. You can provide a clean claim, which means that you come into the office with all of the information that is needed to process your claim. If you cannot go into the Social Security office, *use their Teleclaim Unit.* By calling the office, one of the representatives will take all of this information by phone, and call you back within forty-eight hours to process your application!

You will need:

1. Proof of age.
   a. Certified copy of your birth certificate.
   b. Baptismal record recorded before your fifth birthday.
   Note: If your birth was not recorded in the state or county where you were born, and there is no baptismal record before age five, furnish any of the following documents that show your age or date of birth: school record, census record, children's birth records, insurance policy, marriage license, and church records.

2. Marriage Certificate—certified copy.
   Note: If divorced, provide a copy of the final divorce decree, dates and places of all marriages and all divorces, and the names of the persons you were married to with their social security numbers. If you are over the age of 62, and were married ten years or more, you are entitled to *one-half* of your husband's social security benefits if he/they are alive, and the *full amount* of his/their benefits if deceased.

3. Death certificate (certified copy if you are filing a survivor claim).

4. Proof of burial expenses. If paid in full you will need the receipt when filing for the death benefit.

5. Proof of the court appointment if you are a legal representative.
6. Proof of military service if it applies to you or your husband.
7. Proof of earnings for 1982–83 if you file in 1984. This includes W-2 forms and schedule SE of your tax return. If the forms are not available, have an estimate of the total earnings in wages, and the total *net* earnings if you are self-employed.
8. Bring an estimate of your 1984 earnings, including any vacation pay that is due you in 1984.
9. Worker's compensation notices, including the claim numbers and names and addresses of the insurance companies.
10. Your social security card.
11. If you owned a business and sold it, bring proof of the sale.
12. Social Security will *not* accept copies of any of the above, so *please* bring all original documents. These documents will be promptly returned to you.

Q: What is the date of my entitlement?
A: The month you reach the age of 65. If your birthday is on the first or second of the month you will get paid in that month. If your birthday falls on the third or later you will get your first check the following month.

Q: If I remarry, will I lose my social security benefit check?
A: *Widowed Women:* No, you will not lose any of your benefits. After you are married one year, you will get one-half of your new husband's benefits or your old benefits, whichever are higher, providing you are 62 years of age or older.
Divorced Women: If you are 62 years of age or older and were married ten years or more, you are now receiving one-half of your previous husband's benefits or 100 percent if he is deceased. When you remarry, you will be entitled to one-half of your new husband's social security benefits or keeping the old benefits, whichever is higher.

Q: When do the survivor benefits begin?
A: Widows and widowers of deceased workers are eligible for survivor benefits at the age of 60, and will get this permanently lower payment unless they can wait until they are 65, at which time they will collect the full benefit rate.

Q: How much will I get for a dependent child?

A: Additional benefits for dependent children are 50 percent of the retired worker's benefits and cease when the child turns 18. They can continue fourteen to fifteen months longer if the child is finishing a high school term.

Q: How much will I get for a dependent disabled child?

A: Additional benefits for disabled children are 50 percent of the retired worker's benefits. The child must have been disabled before the age of 22, and the benefits continued during disability.

Q: I will be 65 this year and would like to know how big my social security check will be.

A: Here is what you will get each month if you are claiming your social security benefits at the age of 65 or older. For example, if you turn 65 this year and your average monthly wage was $500, your monthly benefits would be $371; if your average monthly wage was $1,000, your monthly benefits would be $590; and for an average monthly wage of $1,387, your monthly benefits would be the maximum, $709.

Q: How much will I be penalized if I start my benefits when I reach the age of 62?

A: If you retire as early as 62, you will get partial retirement benefits, and you will have to keep that lower benefit for the rest of your life. This amount is 80 percent of the full benefits you would get at age 65. You can, however, work after you retire and still collect some social security benefits, but they will be reduced $1 for every $2 you earn beyond a certain point. That point is $5,160 if you are between the age of 62 to 65, and $6,960 between the ages of 65 and 70. Thereafter you can earn as much as you can without a reduction.

It is very important that you have a statement of your or your husband's social security record of earnings. This record is what the earnings and benefits are based on. Call you local Social Security office and ask them for the preaddressed postcard titled "Request for Social Security Statement of Earnings" form SSA-7004. Fill in your name, address, date of birth, and social security number. Mail it in and get back the information that is so *vital* to your future!

YOUR RIGHT TO APPEAL
UNDER SOCIAL SECURITY OR MEDICARE

You, or someone in your family are getting social security or Medicare checks, and you receive a notice in the mail that your checks are going to be reduced or stopped. Some of you might have a disability claim that is totally denied.

You have been in close contact with a Social Security representative, argued your case with no success, and soon after you get another notice telling you that after *reconsidering* your case you are not entitled to the benefits you feel should be yours. What can you do now?

You have the right to appeal! You can ask for a hearing if you and your representative have disagreed on your claim for benefits.

How to Appeal

If your claim was denied, reconsidered, or revised, request a hearing simply by filling out a "Request for Hearing" form. The forms can be picked up at your local Social Security office. You can also call and ask that one be mailed to you. If you are not able to get this form, write a letter to the Social Security office telling them why you disagree with the decision in your case, enclosing any new evidence that you might have, such as a doctor's opinion if it is a disability claim.

The Hearing

You have a choice as to whether or not you wish to appear. You do not have to be present at the hearing, but in a disability case, it would certainly be to your benefit to appear and testify as to how your disabilities have kept you from working. If a picture is worth a thousand words, then your appearance is worth many times more than any letter you could write.

If you decide against appearing, state your reasons to the representative and ask that the Administration Law judge make the decision based on the material already in your file, plus any new evidence you have to send in.

If your claim is for in-patient hospital care, skilled nursing facilities, or home health care under your Medicare insurance, your claim *must* be over $100. You do not have the right of a hearing if the claim is under $100.

If you are now receiving social security disability benefits, and supplemental security income benefits based on a disability, you are also entitled to request a hearing within sixty days if you are notified that your benefits are being stopped because your medical condition no longer prevents you from engaging in "substantial gainful activity" (going back to work). *Remember* that the sixty days start from the time you receive the notice of the decision to request the hearing. It is presumed that it takes five days from the mailing of the letter to reach you. If you can prove that you did not receive the notice, or show that it was delivered later than the 5 days, you can extend the time.

After you request your hearing, your file is sent to an Administrative Law judge. You will be notified of the date and place the hearing is to be held at least ten days before the hearing.

The hearing could be held within reasonable driving distance of your home, within seventy-five miles of your home, or a greater distance, so that several cases could be heard at one time.

When you are notified of the time and place, if you cannot conveniently travel to that location, *immediately* notify the Adminsitrative Law judge. Your hearing will then be rescheduled closer to your home.

If you are bedridden or unable to travel at that time, a hearing can be held in your home, hospital, institution, or wherever you are. If you cannot travel at all, a doctor's report giving the reasons why you cannot travel would be attached to your "Request for Hearing" form.

The Appeals Council

You now have had your hearing, and you disagree with the Administrative Law judge's findings. You are now entitled to sixty more days (plus the five for mail delivery) to ask for an appeal. You can get this appeal form at your Social Security office (or ask them to mail it to you), or you can write your Social Security office and request a *review* of your case.

The Appeals Council will examine your case and notify you in writing of any action it takes, based on the information in your file, plus any new evidence you sent in with the appeal form.

The Civil Action Suit

If you disagree with the Appeals Council actions—or if the Appeals Council denies your request for a review of the hearing you had earlier with the Administrative Law judge—you can now file a *civil action* in the U.S. District Courts within sixty days (plus the five days for mail delivery). *Note:* If this case involves in-patient hospital care, skilled nursing facilities, or home health services under your Medicare hospital insurance, the amount *must* be over $1,000.

Simplified Steps in Filing an Appeal

1. You have received a notice that your claim is denied or that there will be a reduction in your benefits.
2. You have met with the representative at your local Social Security office, presented your side of the case, and now disagree with their decision.
3. You ask for a hearing with the Administrative Law judge by filling out a "Request for Hearing" form that you get from your local Social Security office.
4. You have had your hearing with the Administrative Law judge, disagree with the findings, and file for an appeal.
5. You file for a Civil Action in a United States District Court.

Time Limit: You have sixty days from the date you receive the notice of a decision in your case. The date of receipt is presumed to be five days after the notice is mailed, unless you can show that you did not receive the notice or can show that it was received later. This time may be extended if there is a good reason.

SUPPLEMENTAL SECURITY INCOME (SSI): WHAT YOU SHOULD KNOW ABOUT IT AND HOW TO OBTAIN IT

Supplemental Security Income (SSI) is a federal program under the guidelines of Social Security that guarantees a certain minimum monthly income to any person over the age of 65, or any person who is blind or disabled at any age.

Can You Qualify?

If you meet one of the above qualifications, and you have no income at all, you could get a monthly check for at least $238.

If you are getting a social security check, the first $20 is subtracted from that check to calculate your income. If you are working, more than half of what you earn could be waived.

You can even own your own home and a car, and still be eligible for SSI. A married person can have other income and resources up to $2250 (a single person up to $1500) and still be eligible. The resources could be assets such as life insurance, stocks, bonds, or property.

Since SSI is based on income and resources, and because some income and resources can be excluded, you will have to do the following: Go to your Social Security office and obtain an application for Supplemental Security benefits. Ask for the booklet on SSI published by the Department of Health and Human Services, or the one published by the National Senior Citizens Law Center to help you better understand your rights.

The Social Security official may tell you that you are not eligible, but fill out the written application anyway and give it to the office manager. If you are denied SSI, you have the right to appeal. The law says that the Social Security office must give you all of the information you need to get SSI, and to explain how you can file an appeal.

If you still feel that you are entitled to SSI and are not getting it, turn for assistance to a lawyer connected with a legal service for low-income families. This lawyer may find a mistake that disqualified you. You may have received mistaken advice through the Family Service Senior Association, the Human Care Services, or your local Senior Citizens Association.

Even if you live in a retirement home, you may be eligible for SSI. Talk to your local Senior Center, your church organization, or your County Agency on Aging. They will have the information on eligibility for these benefits.

First, however, start with your local Social Security office, and if you cannot go there in person, a friend or family member can go for you. Ask for a full explanation of the SSI benefits and get the booklets on SSI. Make out the application and start the wheels turning for that extra retirement help you may be entitled to receive every month!

Receiving Your SSI Checks

Your SSI payments are made by a U.S. government check. The checks are gold colored. Your notice of eligibility explains when your checks will begin and in what amount.

Your check should arrive in the mail about the same time each month, usually at the beginning of the month. If your check is not delivered on the usual date, wait a couple of days, and then get in touch with your Social Security office.

Caution: Never sign your check unless you are ready to cash it. If you sign your check ahead of time and lose it, the person who finds it can cash it. Even though your check can be replaced if it is lost, stolen, or destroyed, you will have to wait a few months to get another one.

HOSPITAL AND MEDICARE MADE SIMPLE

For the senior woman on a limited income, the three greatest concerns are health care, nursing care, and the possibility of a long illness. If you face any of these three, here is information to help you cope.

Let's start with the hospital. The average hospital stay is five to six days. When you check in, Medicare will pay everything except for the $304 deductible. If you must stay sixty-one to ninety days, Medicare will pay all charges except $76 per day. Medicare will pay your first twenty days after which you pay $38 per day at a nursing home, providing you have to stay over twenty days (but not over eighty days). Beyond 100 days you will have to pay all of the charges.

If you have ever seen a bill from a hospital to Medicare, you will realize how much the government is giving you.

Suppose that you do not want to pay the $304 deductible when you check in, or the 20 percent charge Medicare does not pay the doctor. What can you do? You can buy Supplemental Medicare insurance. First, however, call your local Social Security office and ask them to send you the "Guide to Health Insurance for People with Medicare." This pamphlet will give you the useful information for puchasing this supplemental insurance. If you need further assistance, your County Agency on Aging will refer you to an appropriate office to advise you on private insurance policies.

If you decide to buy supplemental insurance, check with your Social Security office to see if you are eligible for Supplemental Security Income (SSI) or any welfare assistance, as your state will protect you over and above the allowed benefits with Medicare.

If you have a medical condition that requires frequent visits and treatment for a long time, ask your doctor to "accept assignment." This means that the doctor will send your bill to Medicare, and accepts whatever Medicare pays.

Suppose that you have been to the doctor, been in the hospital, and are now recuperating for twenty days in a nursing home. The government has already given you thousands of dollars! The doctor then says that you need treatment at home—treatment that you cannot do for yourself. Is there more help available? Yes— your doctor must call the Visiting Nurse Association (VNA). This is a nonprofit group, comprised of registered nurses, therapists, and social workers acting as a team.

The nurses make house calls, not only to give the prescribed treatment, but also to assess the problems of the shut-in. This help includes checking for possible safety hazards and giving instructions in the importance of independence. Often, they help to educate the entire family about medical care.

If the visiting nurse finds the patient too chronically ill to cope with living at home, the patient is referred to nursing facilities or an adult day care program. The charges for visiting nurse care are set by Medicare and paid by Medicare. If the need is beyond the payments allowed by Medicare policy, then the VNA turns to a funding service—The United Way.

The patient must be referred by the hospital, a doctor, or another agency. If, for instance, you need a daily injection, your doctor would give the VNA the prescription and orders.

The Visiting Nurse Association is nationwide, and the doctor, hospital, or the clinic will know if the visiting nurse can be ordered in your area. In some counties, however, the care of the homebound and the families of shut-ins falls to other organizations. The doctor, the out-patient clinic, and the social service department can all direct you to home nursing care.

The government gives you money—and saves you money—in the event of chronic or temporary need in your home!

NEW CHANGES IN MEDICARE

Congress has recently passed a new law that will make some important changes in the Medicare programs. Some of the changes are designed to help the Medicare Administration control their increasing costs, make the program more efficient, and find better ways to deliver their health care to the people who need their services.

Here are some of the changes that will directly affect us:

Hospice Care

Starting November 1, 1983, for a period of three years, Congress authorized hospice care for beneficiaries whose life expectancy is six months or less. This is covered under the Medicare hospital insurance (Part A).

A hospice is a specialized care center for the terminally ill, where patients can elect to go for the treatment and care they need.

The wide range of services that can be covered at a hospice center are nursing care, physical and occupational therapy, speech-language pathology, out-patient drugs for pain relief, homemaker/home health aide services, medical social services, short-term in-patient care, counseling, and respite care (temporary relief for a member of the family performing nursing care).

Workers of Ages 65 to 69

Currently, an employee who is covered by the employer's health insurance becomes eligible for Medicare at the age of 65. At that time, the employer either eliminates from the group plan the benefits that could actually be paid by Medicare, or instead offers a policy that supplements Medicare. This new law now requires all employers of twenty or more people to offer these employees and their spouses aged 65 through 69 any health insurance plan that they are offering to their younger employees, *and* under the same conditions. The employers can offer a policy to supplement Medicare, but it would be for a more limited degree than before.

Again, this means that if you continue to work after the age of

65 you are now able to choose the insurance protection that seems best for you—the plan your employer is offering to all the employees (which Medicare will supplement) or Medicare as your primary coverage.

Payments to Radiologists and Pathologists

In the past, if you were an in-patient in a hospital and received services from a radiologist or a pathologist who accepted the assignment for all such services provided to Medicare in-patients in the hospital, Medicare paid 100 percent of the approved charges. Medicare now pays only 80 percent of the approved charge (after your Part B deductible has been met), and you are responsible for the remaining 20 percent.

Medicare Coverage for Federal Employees

In the past, federal employees did not qualify for Medicare coverage because they were not subject to Social Security tax. Federal employees are now entitled to earn credits toward and qualify for Medicare by paying the Medicare (Part A) hospital insurance portion of the Social Security tax (1.3 percent of their annual wages up to the maximum wage base covered by Social Security).

Full Medicare protection is available on the basis of age, disability, or end-stage renal disease.

Spouses and disabled adult children may also qualify for Medicare. If you are a federal employee you are able to receive credit toward your Medicare eligibility for past federal employment.

HOW FARM INCOME AFFECTS
YOUR SOCIAL SECURITY BENEFITS

The social security benefits that you are now receiving will *not* be reduced if you have rental income from farm property that you own *unless* you actively participate in the management of the farm or in the production of it, which would be spelled out in your rental agreement.

If you help in the running of your farm (the Social Security Administration calls it *materially participating*), you will have to include it in figuring your net earnings from self-employment and report it on your federal income tax returns. Remember, however, that in 1983 you can earn up to $6,600 and not lose any benefits if you are 65 years of age or older.

Farm income can also come from renting or leasing land to another person (regardless of whether you own the land or lease it from somebody else).

Here are the tests to determine whether or not you have materially participated in the rental agreement. These tests are from the official publication of the U.S. Treasury Department:

The Rental Agreement

This is the document you draw up between your tenant and yourself. No two farm rental arrangements are exactly alike; however, all are basically similar in that the farm landlord (you) agrees to permit the tenant the use of the farm to produce farm products. You might also rent it for grazing or pasturing of someone else's livestock on your land.

The tenant agrees to pay the farm landlord for the use of the property either in cash or in a crop share.

The arrangement between you and your tenant may be oral or written. An advantage of a written arrangement is that it makes it easier to establish if the agreement intended for you to materially participate in the farming operation. If the arrangement is oral, it may be necessary to obtain statements from your tenant and others who know the facts about how the two of you had planned to operate.

It's up to you as the landlord to decide on the terms of the arrangement between you and the tenant. If the income, however, is to count for social security, the arrangement must provide for you to *materially participate*. The tests for material participation are as follows:

Test 1

If, as provided for in your arrangement, you do any three of the following four activities, you are materially participating, and your farm rental income *counts for social security:*

a. *Inspect Production Activities.* You meet this part of Test 1 if you inspect the farm from time to time to see if the farm work is being done properly. What was previously ordered is being done, or to decide when various parts of the work should be finished.

Your inspections do not count toward material participation if you only inspect the condition of your farm property or improvements to it, such as buildings, fences, or similar items. The number of inspections you need to make for this part of the test to count is determined by the size and kind of farm you have. Inspections during the plowing, planting, cultivating, and harvesting seasons *will* count.

b. *Tenant Consultations.* Consulting and advising your tenant as to where or how farm commodities are to be produced count toward your material participation.

If you consult, for example, on planting, cultivating, and harvesting, discussing such things as the type of seed to use, how much spraying and fertilizing to do, when and for what amount the crop should be sold, you meet this part of the test.

c. *Furnishing Tools, Equipment, or Livestock.* If you furnish at least half of the tools, equipment, and livestock used in producing the farm commodities, you furnish a significant part—and you meet this part of Test 1.

d. *Share Production Expenses.* If you are responsible for paying at least half of the production costs, you meet this part of the test. It probably would not be considered significant if you were responsible for paying only one-fifth or less of the production costs (whether an amount between a fifth and a half would be significant depends on all the facts).

Production costs include those expenses that relate directly to production of farm commodities—such as cost of feed, seed, plants, fertilizer, fuel, machinery repair, pesticides, and other supplies.

Do not count these items in deciding whether you are materially participating: living expenses of the tenant and the family, the value of the work furnished by the tenant and the family, overhead expenses such as depreciation and taxes.

Test 2—Making Decisions

You are materially participating if, under the arrangement with your tenant, you make decisions on a regular and frequent basis that significantly affect the success of the farm operation. Decisions which count include deciding when to plant, cultivate, dust, spray, or harvest the crop; what goods to buy, sell, or rent, what farming standards to follow, what records to keep, when and how bills are to be paid.

Note: You do not meet Test 2 if you only decide what crops and livestock to raise, where to plant, and what land to leave idle.

Test 3—Taking Part in the Work

You materially participate if, under your rental arrangement, you work at least 100 hours, spread over five or more weeks on activities connected with crop production. The weeks in which you work need not be consecutive, and even if you do nothing else, you are materially participating if you do this amount of work.

Work of fewer than 100 hours, or work in fewer than five weeks, may be called material participation if your efforts add up to a significant contribution to crop production. If your work by itself is not enough to establish material participation—it should be considered along with the other ways you are participating.

Examples of the kinds of work that count include cultivating, harvesting, making purchases, keeping records, caring for livestock, and repairing buildings, fences, and farm equipment used in connection with the crop production.

Remember: Any work you do that is not called for in your rental agreement does not count toward material participation. For example, any work you do under a separate agreement with your tenant to work part time as an employee will *not* count.

Test 4—The Combination of Factors

The first three tests are based on the more common activities of farm landlords. (The word *Landlords* used here means anyone who rents or leases land to another person, regardless of whether he or she owns the land or rents or leases it from someone else.) Even if you do meet Test 1, 2, or 3, your activities when considered together may be a material participation in the farm process and operation. If you are not sure if you are materially participating, ask your local Social Security office or your Internal Revenue Service office for a decision.

A Few Examples

Della C. lives about 100 miles from her farm and under the arrangement with her tenant, her brother who lives near the farm makes all of the important management decisions affecting the crop production. He consults with the tenant on some matters, but regularly and frequently makes the decisions himself. Several times a year he talks with his sister's tenant about the kinds of crops to raise and when they should be harvested. Della C. is not materially participating. Even though her brother has the right to make decisions, she must make these decisions *herself* to qualify.

Landlord Richard L. has his farm run by sharecroppers. He gets half of the crop and furnishes half of the tools and equipment. Under the terms of the rental agreement, Richard L. looks over the progress of the crop often and tells the sharecroppers how they should do the work and where and when each should be planted, and he inspects the production activities regularly during the crop year.

Richard L. *is* materially participating. He tells the sharecroppers how to do the work, inspects the crop from time to time, and furnishes half of the tools and equipment. He meets Test 1, and the farm income that he receives counts toward social security. He would also be materially participating if he did not provide any equipment but paid or stood good for half or more of the cost of producing the crop.

26

TAXES

PROPERTY TAX ASSISTANCE
FOR SENIOR CITIZENS
AND BLIND/DISABLED PERSONS

If you own your own home and find the property taxes nibbling away at spendable income, you can get help from your state. Different states have different eligibility requirements, but here is a simple example of what one state permitted:

An elderly couple who had lived all their lives in a beloved home could not pay their taxes out of their income. With inflation, they had to dip into their savings account to pay the property taxes, and gradually diminished their capital and interest income.

They looked into Property Tax Postponement and found they were eligible in their state. They met the following requirements:

1. They were both over the age of 62.
2. The household income was less than $33,600 a year.
3. The house was the principle place of residence.
4. More than 20 percent of the appraised valuation had been paid off, minus the existing mortgage.

This couple was paying about $2,000 a year in taxes, and now the state is paying their taxes!

The Gonsalves-Deukmejian-Petris Senior Citizens Property Tax Assistance Law provides direct cash reimbursement for part of the property taxes on the homes of qualified persons with total household incomes of $12,000 or less for those who are either 62 or older or blind or disabled.

The filing period for claims for assistance runs from May 16 through August 31. A claim form must be filed each year in order for the cash reimbursement to be received. Filing for property tax assistance does not reduce the amount of property taxes owed to the county tax collector, nor will it result in a lien being placed on the property.

Claim forms and information regarding the Property Tax Assistance Program may be obtained by telephoning your Franchise Tax Board (toll-free).

Property Tax Postponement for Senior Citizens

The Senior Citizens Property Tax Postponement Law gives qualified persons who are 62 or older with a household income of $33,000 or less the option of having the state pay all or part of the taxes on their homes. The amount of taxes postponed must be repaid to the state when the individual moves, sells the property, or dies. The filing period for claims of postponement of taxes, runs from May 17 through December 10, of that year.

A claim form must be filed each year that the individual desires to have property taxes postponed.

Individuals who qualify for postponement may also qualify for property tax assistance!

Claim forms and information regarding property tax postponement may be obtained by telephoning your state controller's office (toll-free).

TAX ADVANTAGES FOR SENIORS

Homes

If you are over 55 years old and sell for $179,000 a home that you bought for $50,000—you get back the $50,000, keep $125,000 of the profit you made—and pay taxes only on $4,000! Even if you are in a 50% tax bracket, the $125,000 is yours to keep. This is a law change for seniors over 55 years old, and it is called the $125,000 Tax Exclusion Gain. You won't have to reinvest this gain, providing you lived in the house for three of the five (or more) years you owned it.

The reinvestment time for all other home sales is eighteen months and is two years from the sale of your old home if you build a new home. *Warning:* You will get into trouble if you sell a home after owning it for only six months, buy another, and sell that one in six months. The middle sale will not count for reinvestment. During an eighteen-month period, you are only allowed one exclusion.

Investments

Tax-free or tax-exempt refers generally to income generated by an investment that will not be taxed, usually due to a specific legal exemption. An example is income generated by a municipal bond.

Tax-deferred refers to income that will be taxed at some point, but not at this time. For example, a series EE savings bond continually earns interest, but it would only be fully taxable when the owner decides to start receiving the income.

Tax-deductible losses or tax deductions can, for example, refer to rental property. If your expenses, such as interest in a loan payment, exceeded the amount of rent you receive, this would be a tax-deductible loss.

Employees' Tax-Free Retirement Fund

The lump sum you receive from a tax-qualified retirement can be transferred to an Individual Retirement Account (IRA). This permits you to postpone federal income tax until the time you wish to withdraw it from the IRA. To qualify for this benefit, the lump sum distribution must meet certain requirements and be made within sixty days of the receipt of your money.

Tax-Exempt Market Funds

If you are seeking relief from an oncoming tax burden, and need the highest degree of liquidity and stability, you might wish to consider investing in a tax-exempt money market fund. Briefly, this type of fund consists of high quality, tax-exempt municipal obligations with short-time maturities. Tax-free dividends are declared daily and reinvested in additional fund shares. Withdrawals can be made by mail, check, telephone, or wire, depending on the rules of the fund. You usually can convert all or part of your account to cash at any time without charge or a withdrawal penalty.

Individual Retirement Accounts (IRA)

If you are earning income and have not reached the age of 70½, you are eligible to contribute your earned income, up to a maximum of $2,000 a year, to your individual retirement account and take a federal income tax deduction for the amount of your contribution. This applies even if you are already covered by another retirement plan. All earnings on these funds are fully tax-deferred until you are retired and begin to withdraw your funds. At that time you will be in a much lower tax bracket and will not have to pay the higher tax rate.

If you are married and your spouse is *not* working, you may be eligible to make a tax-deductible contribution up to $2,250 a year to your IRA joint account. If your spouse *is* working, and you both have earned income, you may each be eligible to set up an Individual Retirement Account (IRA), for a maximum deductible contribution of $4,000 on your joint returns.

Self-Employed Tax Deferrment

Two types of retirement programs are available for self-employed individuals and businesses that are unincorporated, a Keogh (HR-L) or an IRA Simplified Employees Pension (IRA-SEP). Both plans allow you to contribute up to 15 percent of your earned income or $15,000—whichever is less for the year, and to take a tax deduction for the full amount of your contribution.

All of the taxes on your dividends, interest or capital gains in this plan would be deferred. Distributions from a Keogh may be taxed at a lower federal income tax rate when it is distributed to you in a lump sum.

27

TAKING CARE
OF YOUR MONEY

CHECKING ACCOUNT TIPS

Here are a few good tips to remember if you have a checking account:

1. Never endorse a check for deposit until you are at the bank.
2. Always write "for deposit only" after your signature, as a check endorsed in blank is a bearer item, and can be as good as cash to anyone who presents it to the bank for payment.
3. Never keep any identification or credit cards in your checkbook. Many women tuck these cards in the flap of their checkbook to keep them handy for identification, but they are too easily lost, and when lost, take months of trouble to replace.
4. Check your bank statements as you get them monthly, always making sure that your deposits are correct, the balance is right, the amounts are correct—and most important of all—see if those checks belong to you!

USING DIRECT DEPOSIT

According to the Department of Treasury, over six million Americans have already begun using direct deposit which allows you to have your monthly government check delivered directly to your savings institution.

Whether your benefits are from social security, Supplemental Security Income, railroad retirement, civil service retirement, or Veterans Administration Compensation and Pension plan, you are eligible for this voluntary government program.

Here is an ideal way to handle this precious check that comes to us once a month. You won't have to stay at home and wait for the mailman to show up. Impossible weather conditions won't affect the delivery of your money. No more worries about a check loss through theft or forgery, and if you are sick or disabled, you won't have to go out to make that trip to the bank!

Let direct deposit work for you. Take your next check to your bank, savings bank, savings and loan institution, or state-chartered credit union, and tell them that you want to sign up for direct deposit. They will help you to complete the form and will give you a copy of it.

Within ninety days Uncle Sam will begin depositing your benefit check directly into your personal checking or savings account on the payment date.

If there is a change in your payment amount, or if the government has any general information important for you to know, this information will be sent direct to you at your home.

Questions about your benefit or retirement status will continue to be handled by the appropriate government agency (Social Security Administration, Railroad Retirement Board, Civil Service Commission, or Veterans Administration).

With direct deposit you may:

1. Choose the financial organization to which your payment will be sent.
2. Choose the account in which your payments will be deposited.
3. Cancel direct deposit at any time and begin receiving your payments at home again.
4. Change the financial organization if you so desire.

Here are some comments from people who are using this service:

"We are participating in the direct deposit program and believe it is a great improvement over the former program of mailing checks."

"It is certainly a wonderful convenience to receive uninterrupted deposits and to eliminate check loss, theft, and forgery. I signed up for it the very first month."

"I wish that every senior citizen could enjoy such carefree handling of precious and not-too-plentiful funds. I have never had a worry."

There is no charge for this service, and many savings institutions offer free checking service to senior citizens who utilize the Direct Deposit System.

28

STARTING YOUR OWN BUSINESS WITH HELP FROM THE SMALL BUSINESS ADMINISTRATION

The attraction of owning your own business is strong—being your own boss and seeing the immediate results of your own efforts. To develop your own company and be independent is a very exciting prospect.

The Small Business Administration might be just what you are looking for.

If you are beginning to grow a little, and have found something that you like to do (and it's making a little money for you), you might want to expand.

Women are entitled to all of the many services of the Small Business Administration (SBA) without prejudice or discrimination. Too few women are taking advantage of the opportunities that exist in local SBA offices, and if you are a woman considering going into business, or a woman already in business who is in financial difficulties, the SBA is issuing you a personal invitation to find out what they can do for you.

If you go to a bank or a lending institution to apply for a loan, here are some of the questions that you will be asked: What kind of a business are you thinking of going into? How much money do you have to invest in the new venture? What experience do you have that makes you think you can succeed in business? Have you surveyed the market you plan to enter? Have you chosen a location? How much money will you need to borrow? What will the money be used for and what collateral can you offer to prove you will repay the loan?

If you cannot establish a sufficient credit background to qualify for a loan from a conventional lender (bank, savings and loan institution, credit union, or other lender), the SBA could provide this assistance through a variety of loan programs. You must, however, show proof that you have been turned down by a commercial lender (two in a city of over 200,000) before you can apply to the SBA for the help that you need.

Most SBA loans are either guaranteed by a bank for 90 percent of the loan or they are loans made by a participation with other commercial lenders.

The greatest single problem most women face in entering business is the establishment of credit to meet their initial requirements. With the initiation of the National Women's Business Ownership Campaign, an increase in the percentage of loans the Small Business Administration made or guaranteed to women is becoming apparent. In fiscal year 1974, women received only 7 percent of all SBA loans. In fiscal year 1979, however, the SBA made 4,800 loans to women, which was 16 percent of all the loans they issued. The dollar amount was $380 million.

Do get in touch with your nearest SBA office as soon as you begin to see what it might take for you to start your own business (or enlarge the one you already have). Tell them that you want to go into business. Ask for some of their "starting up" publications:

1. SMA 17 "Checklist for Going into Business."
2. SMA 150 "Business Plan for Retailers."
3. SMA 153 "Business Plan for Small Business Firms."
4. SMA 170 "Thinking about Going into Business?"
5. SMA 218 "Business Plan for Small Manufacturers."
6. SMA 221 "Business Plan for Small Construction Firms."
7. SBA 115-A Lists of free SBA publications.
8. SBA 115-B Lists of "For Sale" booklets *plus* a "Request for Counseling" form.

The two most important materials, according to the SBA, are the first and last. The significance of "Worksheet #2," which is the centerfold of the 17 "Checklist," cannot be overemphasized. Do not guess. Take your time and get the answers from people who can advise you.

Sign the "Request for Counseling" form and mail it or take it to the SBA. The counseling is a wonderful business service offered by a service corps of retired executives that call their business management counseling "SCORE," which stands for "Service Corps of Retired Executives."

SCORE is a group of men and women who offer their successful experiences in management ventures. They advise about starting a new business, how to manage or merchandise the new venture and how to upgrade the management of an existing business (if you have already started and might need help).

This service is nationwide, and without charge, so take advantage of this wonderful opportunity. The SCORE counselors are business-oriented men and women from all walks of life. There are more than 12,000 in the nation who volunteer solely for the purpose of helping you become more successful.

When you mail or take in your "Request for Counseling" form, ask your counselor to visit you at your home or business. They will give you the best impartial advice that they can.

At this time, the SBA loan program is primarily centered around their loan guarantee program. This means that the SBA acts as a guarantor to the bank in case of default of a small business loan that was guaranteed by the federal government. Prepare you business plan and loan application in accordance with the required outline. You can obtain this application from your business counselor in the SBA. Then take it to your bank and apply for a loan. If they are unwilling to consider your application for a loan, take it to another bank. Then, if you are once more refused a loan, you are now eligible to apply to the SBA for a direct loan.

Every community needs people who can take an idea and work it into a small business that will be both profitable and rewarding. A growing economy is a good time for you to create something for yourself that will give you the independence you need.

No question that you want to ask the SBA is too small or unimportant. Don't be shy about asking questions that you think are "dumb." The more questions you ask, the more you show a willingness to find the information that will help you succeed.

After you plan to open your new business, you can enroll in two different SBA management assistance courses, a prebusiness workshop, and an advertising/training program. Taking courses in advance planning will benefit you, and the value of the advertising/training course will be evident before your first year in business is finished.

Loans that are made under special circumstances include the following:

Economic Opportunity Loans: Granted to people who are socially and/or economically disadvantaged.

Handicapped Assistance Loans: Granted to physically handicapped small business owners, and to public and private nonprofit organizations that employ and operate in the interest of physically handicapped persons.

Displaced Business Loans: Granted to help firms suffering substantial economic injury due to displacement by federal renewal or other construction projects relocate themselves. A reasonable upgrading of the business at the same time is permitted.

29

A PART-TIME JOB
FROM THE JOBS TRAINING
PARTNERSHIP ACT (JTPA)

The government has been putting *emphasis* on helping older women!

The Job Training Partnership Act (JTPA) was established as a permanent job-training system for the disadvantaged, including the elderly.

The JTPA enlarged the role of the state government and private industry in federal job-training programs and created a new program of retraining displaced workers.

According to President Reagan, this bill is targeted to "one million disadvantaged people," including workers aged 55 and older. The bill sets aside 3 percent of each state's training funds for the older worker. The House of Representatives passed a $4.9 billion package on March 3, 1983. Some of that money could be sifting down to you!

If you are on welfare, SSI, rent assistance, or food stamps, you are eligible for job training. Contact your local CETA center for information regrading job training for you.

Does the word "job" sound like too much work for you? Not under this program, as you will be trained for a job flexible to your needs. You will have special working conditions, flexible hours, or share a half-day with another woman for the same job.

If you are able to do part-time work, or if your income falls under the federal poverty levels, go after the government. You can get the training you need, the job you need, and the money you need!

Appendix A

HELPFUL HINTS FROM YOUR SENIOR CITIZENS ASSOCIATION

As the old saying goes, "May all your troubles only be little ones!"
But little or big, here are a number of places for seniors to call or write to for help in their communities.

1. *Allied Community Services, Inc.:* Supplies homemakers and home health aides. If it has a different name in your community, call your local senior citizens center. Your telephone information service will find the correct numbers for you.

2. *Family Service Senior Association* and *Human Care Service Programs* will help you on money matters, legal problems, consumer rights, counseling and emergencies, health problems and services, nursing care, housing, funeral costs, transportation, clubs and recreation, home helpers and handymen, free blood pressure checks, and reassurance calls and visits. Ask if they have a newsletter. Also: weekly nutrition program, location of hot lunches. Transportation may be available if needed.

3. *Low-Cost Robbery Insurance:* Sold in 28 states. To get detailed information, write Federal Crime Insurance, P.O. Box 41033, Washington, D.C., 20014, or call toll-free 1-800-638-8780.

4. *Foot Clinic:* Some senior centers have bimonthly foot clinics. Ask for transportation or call your state Podiatry Association for a clinic nearby.

5. *Workshops:* Your local branch of Seniors in Action has workshops and programs available for individual participation.

6. *Post-Stroke Patients Club:* Social club for companionship and life enrichement. Ask telephone information or your senior citizens center for the phone number.

7. *Coronary Vascular Accident Club:* Membership participation, meetings include family, speakers, therapists, and movies. Transportation can be arranged.

8. *American Association of Retired Persons (AARP):* Has slides and lectures, can direct you to low-cost travel.

9. *National Association of Retired Federal Employees:* Call them for a monthly program.

10. *The Salvation Army, Senior Center:* Hot lunches, senior activities, day trips, folk dancing, cooking, language lessons, sewing, bingo, films. Also: Telephone reassurance, transportation, and escort service.

11. *Senior Center, Medical Section:* Podiatry, hearing tests, dental exams, heart and eye consultations, arthritis and dermatology exams. Your senior center will tell you where to call for an appointment.

12. *Widows and Widowers Club:* Ask telephone information for the number in your area. Call them and find out about their social events, such as guest speakers, programs, tours, dinners, and dancing.

13. *Physical Fitness:* Call your local chapter of the YMCA (or YWCA) for information on exercise classes and swimming. They usually charge a small fee.

14. *Tax Assistance:* Senior Adult Services or your local senior center can help you with a volunteer assistant.

15. *Free Vegetables and Fruit:* In rural areas your senior center can tell you where to pick up free produce brought by volunteers for senior citizens from the area Agency on Aging.

16. *Self-Defense:* If you are interested in using tear gas (a pocket-size device containing a non-lethal chemical) for self-defense, call the Public Safety Training Association in your area. You can qualify to use it by taking a two-hour class.

17. *Vision Problems:* Touchables, a device with large buttons that slides readily over the phone (about $9) is available by writing for information to Touchables, 207 West Ohio St., Chicago, IL 60610.

18. *Medicare Problems:* If Medicare billing becomes complicated, contact your senior citizens center and ask about medical billing workshops (conducted by volunteers). In some areas you can call Adult Protective Service.

19. *Obscene Telephone Calls:* Show no emotion, say nothing, and hang up quietly. If the calls persist, contact your local telephone business office, where a specialist can take steps to help remedy the problem.

20. *Fixed Income Annuity:* You can increase the income from a nest egg by buying a fixed income annuity. Call any large insurance company or write for a booklet to Arnold I. Kaiser, The Equitable Building, Suite 200, 133 Camino de Rio South, San Diego, CA 92108. You will receive about 11 percent on your investment every month for the rest of your life. You will never outlive your principal, but payments stop at death so you leave no estate.

21. *Hearing Problems:* Write for a free booklet to Bel-Tone Hearing Aid Service, P.O. Box 28626, San Diego, CA 92128. The booklet describes types of hearing problems and how to get help.

22. *Your Retirement and the Law:* The Administration on Aging has a booklet that describes how to go about getting legal advice when you need it. Send $1.20 to Consumer Information Center, Dept. 164 H, Pueblo, CO 81009. You will also receive a free copy of the Consumer Information Catalogue, listing 200 other federal publications to help you.

23. *Beauty and Home Care Productions:* You can save money by making up your own formulas for skin care and housecleaning chores. *The Formula Book* (in paperback) gives you more than 200 recipes and instructions for homemade formulas with simple explanations on ingredients and equipment. Send $5.95 to *The Formula Book,* Universal Press Syndicate, 6700 Squibb Road, Mission, KS 66202.

Appendix B

SUCCESS STORIES

By sharing the experiences, concerns, and successes of other women, this section supports and encourages all women in the labor force and those who are thinking about going into the business world.

There remain few areas of achievement in which women haven't entered and contributed their energies and talents. Most women will work for at least 30 years, even if they take time out to raise children.

Here are a few examples of successful small businesses run by women having some common characteristics. They view themselves as doers with strong desires to achieve. They are goal-setters who are organized, self-motivated, confident, and self-reliant with high energy levels.

Today, a woman's place is *everywhere*. If you have a dream, pursue it! If you want a career, go for it!

1. Ellen lives in a small Midwest town. She has two children, a boy and a girl. It was costly for she and her husband to buy new clothes for each child as they grew out of their old clothes, and she vowed to herself that when she had time she would open a store that sold secondhand good clothing for children for at least half the price (or less) of new clothes. Peo-

ple liked the idea, and she now has a business that caters to the whole family for their clothing needs.

Ellen is enthusiastic about the concept of her new store—turning clothes no longer needed into cold cash. She calls this business "Rag-Time." It is advertised as a clothing brokerage business for new and used clothing. She accepts "like-new" cast-offs: dresses, suits, men's clothing, juniors', children's and infants' wear on a consignment basis and keeps half the proceeds for her share.

She has been open for about a year now, and she explained that it's easy to consign clothes. "Clothing must be in style," says Ellen, and "garments must be laundered or dry cleaned, in excellent condition, on hangers, and their sizes indicated. Not more than fifteen articles of clothing should be consigned at one time." She also advises that bringing in clothes early in the season will give a better chance of selling them.

2. Cathy is married and the mother of two. She had baked and designed cakes in her own home for six years and has now opened up her own business. She calls it "Custom Cakes by Cathy." Her specialty is cake sculpture of any design, in any of fourteen flavors, for parties, weddings, and any extra-special occasions.

3. Ann calls herself the "Wallpaper Doll." She has always had a natural ability to decorate, and, encouraged by her friends, she decided to go into business more than two years ago. Her interest "stems from the desire to make people's homes beautiful and comfortable to live in," she says.

She gives free professional advice—brings all the samples of paper to the customer's home—and still manages to save her customers money. Her secretary and receptionist is her 91-year-old father, who, she says, "flirts with all her female customers."

4. Edna is 65 years old and started a baby-sitting career about a year ago. She found out that there is a great demand for older women to care for children in the parents' home. Many times she stays weekends to give the young parents a chance to go off on a small vacation. She suggests that anyone interested in doing the same thing should inquire at church or a senior community center.

5. Sara and Frank have a three-bedroom home and take care of five live-in elderly people. They all get along and have a good time. Sara learned of an abandoned dog last July and decided that maybe there could be a place for it at their home. After getting a veterinary check-up, Muffin gave up her vagabond lifestyle and moved in. Nourishment and nursing care just aren't enough for their residents, Sara felt. "They need things to stimulate their minds—and Muffin has been able to do this."

6. One woman spoke to her local bakery owner who baked salt-free bread for special customers. Working people on salt-free or sugar-free diets needed home-cooked meals to fit their diets. Arrangements were made for her to provide nutritious diet dinners in the bakery freezer. She has extra money every week now.

7. A local delicatessen serving delicious sandwiches and coffee needed homemade pies and cakes of the same quality. A homemaker now supplies, daily, a big pie and a cake. She and the delicatessen carefully worked out the cost of the ingredients and the cost to the customer per slice. She has her profit and her time is well spent in making extra money.

8. A happy seamstress contacted nursery schools and left her address and phone number there for busy mothers who had no time for mending. She now has bundles to be mended dropped off at her door. The darned socks, the repaired seams, and the newly buttoned shirts are picked up again, and the money is rolling in!

9. In the spring, they say, a young man's fancy turns to love; but to Barbara, an enterprising woman living in California, it's spring all year around, and romance is no fancy—it's a living! Barbara, 67, runs a love-letter writing service and she says she drew on her personal life experiences to begin this business eight months ago. For $25 she will pound out two pages of dreamy, serious, funny, or pleading words to the person of your dreams.

    "Since I was a little girl, I always wrote back and forth to all of my girlfriends and boyfriends, and now they encouraged me to do this for money, as I'm told that I write pretty good letters," she said. She also says that she can write a better letter if the person reminds her of someone she knows.

10. A lesson from a Vietnamese cook started Lynne making flaky stuffed rolls—a perfect, delicate flavor with predinner cocktails. She now takes orders for dinner parties and club affairs that pay well for these exotic pastries.

11. Jennie designed for her own use a set of washable nylon cord placemats with a silver thread carried through. They were so admired that she now knits them up fast to sell to friends and gift shops.

12. Louise, tired of making large quilts, designed primitives of flowers, birds, and local buildings to quilt. And now, given a snapshot, she will take an order for a primitive of the customer's house. She shows her work at gift shops, art shops, and local bazaars.

13. In a rural area, Erma, a senior woman, started in her own home a "grandmother's closet," where she sells "second time around" children's clothing to delighted mothers. Mothers sell their outgrown children's clothing to her in almost new condition, and inexpensively buy from her clothes to fit. She makes 100 percent profit—or more!

INDEX

A

Aluminum cans, recycling of, 78
Appeals, social security, 169–171
Art, *See* Paintings.

B

Bags, knitted/crocheted bag, 32
Balls, soft play balls, 31–32
Battery car, 157–158
   checking of, 157
   jump-starting, 158
Bayberry candles, 49–50
Beauty, *See* Cosmetology.
Beauty aids, retailing of, 111
Book carrier and cover, 24–25
Boxes, shell craft boxes, 26–27
Business opportunities:
   children's clothing, selling of, 148–149
   cosmetology, 109–113
   crafts for the handicapped, 26–33
   day care centers, 120–122
   decorating, 99–102
   handcrafts, 34–66
   handcrafts business, 135–141
   mail-order businesses, 93–98
   needlework, 15–33
   painting, 103–105
   party plans, 90–92
   plants, rentals, 116–119
   postal service, 106–108
   property management, 128–134
   recycling, 78–79
   renting, 123–127
   resumes, 74–77
   selling, 85–92
   teaching, needlecraft, 146–147
   teaching, sewing, 142–145
   wallpapering, 67–73
Business records, 98

C

Cactus, growing of, 80–82
Candles:
   bayberry, 50–51
   hand-shaped, 49–50
   sandcasting candles, 48–49
Cars:
   battery check, 157
   checking before repairing, 155–158
   jump-starting battery, 158
   lifting hood, 155
   motor oil check, 155–156
   radiator check, 156
   tires check, 156–157
Checking accounts, tips for, 185
Children's clothing, selling discount, 148–149
Collage, 41–43
Consignment, selling on, 139–140
Cork puppy, 63–64
Cosmetology, 109–113
   clientele building, 110
   customer satisfaction, 111
   equipment, 110–111
   financing, 111
   home service, 110
   information sources, 113
   locations, 109
   pampering clients, 112
   retailing beauty aids, 111
   trends, 113
Counseling, business counseling, 190
Coupon wallet, 21–22
Craft fairs, selling at, 140–141
Crafts, *See* Handcrafts.
Crafts for the handicapped, 26–33
   canvas embroidery, 27–29
   clutch purse, 32
   knitted/crocheted bag, 32

Crafts for the handicapped (*cont.*)
  rosette doll, 30–31
  shell craft boxes, 26–27
  soft play ball, 31–32
  square needlework, 31–33
  tips for, 32–33

D

Day care center, 120–122
  for handicapped, 121
  licensing, 122
  methods of starting, 120–121
  services from state offices, 121–122
Decorating, 99–102
  color use, 99–100
  draperies, 100–102
Decoupage, 39–40
Deposits, from tenants, 132–133
Direct deposit, 186–187
Direct mail, 93
  advertising, 97
  letter, 97
Direct marketing, 94
Direct sales, 88–92
  See also Selling.
Dolls, rosette doll, 30–31
Door-to-door selling, 89–90
Draperies, 100–102
  lengths of, 100–101
  rods, 102

E

Electric range, checking before repairing,
  154
Embroidery, canvas, 27–29
Eyeglass case, 17–18

F

Fabric, hand printing on, 51–54
Farm income, social security and, 176–180
  participation criteria, 177–180
  rental agreement, 177
Federal employees, Medicare, 176
Financing:
  cosmetology business, 111
  handcrafts business, 137–138
  mail order business, 95–96
  See also Small Business Administration.
Flocks/foil wallpapers, 68
Flowers, sachets, 34–36

G

Gas stove, checking before repairing, 154
Gingerbread man, party favor, 62–63
Glass painting, 37–39
Government:
  farm income and social security
    benefits, 176–180
  Medicare, 173–176
  social security, 163–173
  taxes, 181–184
  teleservice, 161–162
Government assistance, handcrafts
    business, 137–138

H

Handcrafts, 34–66
  candles, bayberry, 50–51
  candles, sand casting, 48–49
  collage, 39, 41–43
  decoupage, 39–40
  glass painting, 37–39
  handprinting on fabric, 51–54
  hand shaped, 49–50
  leatherwork, 57–60
  papermaking, 60–62
  party favors, 62–65
  placemats, handprinted, 52–54
  pomander balls, 36–37
  sachets, 34–36
  sand casting, 46–49
  seashell crafts, 43–45
  shell-decorated mirrors, 46
  shell necklaces, 45
  weaving, 54–57
Handcrafts business, 135–141
  craft fairs, 140–141
  equipment/materials, 136–137
  financing, 137–138
  government assistance, 137–138
  home production, 136
  market factors, 136
  pricing, 138–139
  sales representation, 138
  selling on consignment, 139–140
  selling retail, 140
  selling wholesale, 139
  street exhibits, 141
  studio help, 138
Handicapped, *See* Crafts for the
    handicapped.

Hand printing on fabric, 51–54
  placemats, 52–54
Hand-shaped candles, 49–50
Homes:
  cosmetology business, 110
  day care centers, 120–122
  handcrafts business, 36
  renting parts of, 123–127
  tax advantages for elderly, 182–183
Hospice care, Medicare, 173–176

I

Illness, *See* Medicare.
Individual Retirement Accounts (IRA), 184
Investments, tax advantages, 183

J

Job Training Partnership Act (JTPA), 192

L

Leases, 131–132
Leatherwork, 57–60
  decorating leather, 59–60
  patterns, 58–59
  types of leather, 57–58
Letters, motivation letter, 76–77
Licenses:
  day care center, 122
  selling, 85
Loom, use in weaving, 55–57

M

Mail-order business, 93–98
  advertising, 97
  business records, 98
  capital needed, 95
  choosing products, 96
  components of, 93
  financing arrangements, 95–96
  legal requirements, 94–95
  products for resale, 96–97
  starting of, 94–96
Management, property management,
  128–134
Marketing:
  direct marketing, 94
  mail order, 93–94

Medicare, 173–176
  federal employees, 176
  hospice care, 175
  radiologist/pathologist payments, 176
  workers ages 65–69, 175–176
Mitten duster, knitted, 15–17
Money market, tax-exempt market funds,
  183–184
Money matters:
  checking accounts, 185
  direct deposit, 186–187
Moth-protection, sachets for, 35–36
Motor oil, checking of, 155–156
Murals, wallpaper, 69

N

Napkin holders, 20–21
  place mat purses, 23–24

P

Plants:
  cactus, growing of, 80–82
  hanging plants, 117
  interior plantscaping, 114–115
  potted floor plants, 117–118
  renting of, 116–119
Pomander balls, 36–37
Postal service, 106–108
  locations for, 107
  optional services, 107–108
  rates, 106
Prepasted wallpaper, 72
Products:
  advertising, 97
  mail order business and, 96
  for resale, 96–97
Property management, 128–134
  key deposits, 133
  late-paying tenants, 132
  learning business of, 129
  leases, 131–132
  management fees, 133–134
  pet deposits, 133
  rent pricing, 130
  security deposits, 133
  showing apartments, 130–131
  tenant information, 131
Property Tax Assistance Law, 182
Property Tax Postponement Law, 181, 182

Purses:
  clutch, 32
  place mat purses, 23–24

R

Radiator, checking in car, 156
Real estate, property management, 128–134
Records, keeping business records, 98
Recycling, 78–79
  aluminum cans, 78
  paper, 79
Refrigerator, checking before repairing,
    153–154
Remnant space, 97
Renting, 123–127
  client information, 124
  entrance renovation, 126
  financing for renovation, 126–127
  pitfalls of, 124–125
  plumbing and renovation, 126
  property management, 128–134
  types of, 123
  weekly rates, 124
  zoning and, 125–126
Resumes, 74–77
  information for, 74–75
  motivation letter, 76–77
Retirement, tax-free retirement fund, 183
Rosette doll, 30–31

S

Sachets:
  flower garden sachets, 34–36
  for moth protection, 35–36
Sandcasting, 46–49
  candles, 48–49
Saving:
  on appliance repairs, 153–154
  on car repairs, 155–158
SCORE, business counseling, 190
Seashell crafts, 43–46
  boxes, 26–27
  mirrors, shell-decorated, 46
  necklaces, 45
  preparation of shells, 43–45
Self-employment:
  self-employed tax deferrment, 184
  See also Business opportunities.
Selling, 85–92
  children's clothing, 148–149
  direct sales, 88–92
  direct sales firms, 92

Selling *(cont.)*
  door-to-door selling, 89–90
  getting orders, 87
  handcrafts business, 135–141
  license for, 85
  party plans, 90–92
  price decision, 86–87
  retail, 140
  self-promotion, 87
  wholesale, 139
Senior citizens:
  associations for, 193–195
  social security, 163–173
  tax advantages for, 182–184
Sewing, teaching of, 142–145
  charge for, 143–144
  in cities/mall areas, 143
  pampering students, 144
  in rural areas, 142
  sewing associations, 144–145
  trends and, 144
Slippers, party slippers, 64–65
Small Business Administration (SBA),
    188–191
  important forms, 189–190
  special circumstances for, 191
  starting-up publications, 189
Social security, 163–173
  appeals, 169
  appeals council, 170
  civil action suits, 171
  direct deposit, 186–187
  filing appeals, 171
  hearings for appeals, 169–170
  questions and answers, 163–168
  Supplemental Security Income (SSI),
      171–173
Square needlework, 31–33
Street exhibits, selling at, 141
Supplemental Security Income (SSI),
    171–173
  qualifying for, 172
  receiving checks, 173

T

Taxes, 181–184
  homes, tax advantages, 182–183
  Individual Retirement Accounts (IRA),
      184
  investments, tax advantages, 183
  Property Tax Assistance Law, 182
  Property Tax Postponement Law, 181,
      182

Taxes (*cont.*)
  self-employed tax deferrment, 184
  Tax Exchange Gains, 182–183
  tax-exempt market funds, 183–184
  tax-free retirement fund, 183
Tax Exchange Gain, 182–183
Teaching:
  needlecraft, 146–147
  sewing, 142–145
Teleservice, 161–162
Television, checking before repairing, 153
Tenants:
  property management, 128–134
  renting at home, 123–127
Tires, checking of, 156–157
Typing, resumes, 74–77

V

Vinyl wall coverings, 68

W

Wall papering, 67–73
  choosing wallpaper, 69–70
  flocks/foil papers, 68
  murals/graphics, 69
  ordering wallpaper, 70
  preparation of walls, 73
  prepasted wallpaper, 72
  procedure for, 70–72
  removing old paper, 73
  tools for, 72
  vinyl wall coverings, 68
  woven wall coverings, 69
Weaving, 54–57
Wind socks, 18–20
Women, Small Business Administration
    loans and, 189
Woven wall coverings, 69